Freda's first book shows a cooking should be a part of eve was born of her concern that th family would not get the opportunity of learning to cook. This cookery 'handbook' is the result.

A career that has involved working with food in various guises started with training at Westminster College (Hotel School), Vincent Square, London SW1. Along the way have been positions in hotel management, running hotel and restaurant businesses in partnership with husband Karl - The George and Dragon, Codicote; The White Horse Inn, Hertingfordbury; Ye Olde Welcome, East Grinstead; The Red Lion, Crewkerne and Schaffer's Restaurant, Highcliffe. When times became difficult and with a mortgage to pay, a position of Head Cook/Manager beckoned at the local comprehensive school. This was shortly after school catering was privatised and proved to be a good lesson in economical catering.

In amongst the above experiences she held two positions of chef/lecturer in the hospitality departments of Bournemouth University and Brockenhurst College, Hampshire.

Praise for FAVOURITE FAMILY FOOD

Feeding your family with real home cooking is one of the most rewarding parts of everyday family life.
Freda Schaffer's Favourite Family Food ticks all the boxes from shopping, preparing, time saving tips, food for friends and through to really helpful hints and tips on giving children good food habits. This book will give you everything you need to know to make every day eating a real pleasure.
Lesley Waters - TV celebrity chef and writer.

This book has the food that mum and grandma made, and some new dishes - and practical details on how to prepare and cook them in easy-to-understand form. It is just the thing for people like me who were never taught to cook, and for people who learnt a few dishes but want to put good food from wholesome ingredients on the family table.
Rt.Hon. Sir Alan Beith, M.P.

A wonderful collection of straightforward recipes for everyday eating and comfort food. A complete beginner can follow the step-by-step guidelines, while regular family cooks can find new inspiration.
Roni Jay - publisher and writer.

Freda's book is great for anyone who wants to feed their family well. It is full of simple, practical advice as well as everyday family recipes. I am sure any mum would agree that this is a cookery book which you would want to cook every recipe from, rather than just one or two. It has been invaluable to me in organising a weekly menu of affordable, tasty and nutritious meals that are enjoyed by the entire family. This book has quickly become my everyday companion both in the kitchen and in the supermarket. As I try each new recipe, it becomes yet another family favourite!
Katrina Fox - young mum with family.

FAVOURITE

FAMILY FOOD

HOME COOKING

To Helen,

Happy Cooking!!

from Peter & Susan

FREDA SCHAFFER

Text and illustrations © 2009 Freda Schaffer.

Published by Fresch Publishing.
Contact:enquiries@freschpublishing.com

All rights reserved. No part of this publication may be reproduced, stored in a retrieval system, or transmitted, in any form or by any means without the prior written permission of the publisher.

The author/illustrator asserts her moral right to be identified as author and illustrator in accordance with the Copyright, Designs and Patents Acts 1988.

A CIP catalogue record of this title is available from the British Library.

ISBN 978-0-9564025-0-9

Printed and bound in Great Britain by
CPI Antony Rowe, Chippenham and Eastbourne

For my grandchildren Matthew, Ryan, Aaron, Chloe and Jamie, with love.

ACKNOWLEDGEMENTS

My thanks go to my husband Karl who has been exceptionally supportive throughout the writing of this book. As well as dishing out oodles of encouragement he has capably dished up our meals from Monday to Friday!

Special thanks are also due to Roni Jay who has been an invaluable asset in mentoring me during this period - answering my many queries. Her book 'The White Ladder Diaries' (the pain and pleasure of launching a business) was also extremely helpful.

CONTENTS

MY TOP TEN TIPS	3
COOKING WITH NUMBERS	4
SHOPPING SUGGESTIONS	6
GOOD GEAR FOR THE KITCHEN	7
KEEPING FOOD COLD	13
BEAT THE BUGS	14
TACTICS WITH CHILDREN	15
COOKING FOR ONE - STUDENTS	17
TIME SAVING TIPS	20
ON YOUR MARKS! (Before you start)	23
SOUPS AND SNACKS	24
VEGETABLES, POTATOES, SALADS & DRESSINGS	36
PIZZA, PASTA, RICE, PANCAKES & SAVOURY TARTS	52
MAIN MEALS - FISH & MEAT	66
FOOD FOR FRIENDS	107
SWEETS, PUDDINGS etc.	118
PASTRY, CAKES AND BISCUITS	136

ILLUSTRATIONS

SPOON MEASUREMENTS	5
KNIVES	9
ONIONS	35
TOMATOES, GARLIC, SPRING ONIONS	47
MUSHROOMS	77
PEPPERS	109
HINTS - BAKING	117
DESSERTS AND PASTRY	131
CAKES	141
HINTS - CAKES	153

Introduction

Food glorious food! COOK - EAT - ENJOY!

What is the point of food? What does food do for you? The truth is that it is your *fuel* for living. Feed on poor quality food and your body will retaliate in a variety of ways. The one most important point to remember is that meals prepared with quality, fresh ingredients in your own kitchen will be far superior to any *ready meal.* Cooking for yourself will enable you to have full control over what goes to make up your meals.

We must dispel the illusion that cooking is time consuming. Also let us ignore the following - quick, easy, ready in ten minutes and many more ambiguous claims. The secret of successful, stress-free cooking can be summed up as P&O - no not a shipping company but *preparation and organisation.* If you are starting a meal from scratch when you arrive home from college, university, work etc. you are certainly not approaching home cooking from the right angle. Much can be prepared beforehand and organisation of your time is vital. It has nothing to do with how quickly you can *throw things together.*

This collection of recipes includes some from my Mother together with favourites of my own and are ideal for everyday home cooking. I am dedicating this book to my grandchildren in the hope that they will experience pleasure from cooking and eating good food as I have done, not only within the bounds of my own family, but also amongst friends. Good food unites and holds families together. I recollect many happy family gatherings around the table and especially when my children were in their teens. I am sure that they experienced other *pulls* but I was thrilled to find that, whatever else was going on, they always appeared for a roast on a Sunday.

Cooking doesn't come easily to us all but with good common sense acceptable results are definitely achievable. Most savoury recipes will tolerate approximations and other ingredients can often be left out or added. An exception to this is baking - *bread, pastries, cakes, sweets etc.,* where exact quantities are usually essential.

I have no doubt that my mother's influence made me the cook that I am today. Apart from being a wonderful cook she allowed me to assist and experiment in the kitchen as well as being extremely tolerant of the mess I created. On arriving home from school wonderful smells would be coming from the kitchen - appetising dishes that were being prepared for myself and my sister. At the time I did not fully appreciate my Mother's endeavours to any great degree, taste wise yes but work wise no. I now realise what satisfaction she must have gained from feeding us fresh and tasty food and I certainly look back on those times with much warmth and gratitude. Thankfully we can do the same but with a lot more help from electrical gadgets and ready prepared sauces, soups, flavourings etc.

Encourage your children to cook at a young age - they will love it. Patience you will need. Rewards will be great. Kids are so proud of any achievement in cooking. This gesture will be a small contribution from you in helping your children to grasp a most important life skill.

My Top Ten Tips - plus one.

1. Wash hands before you start cooking and in between when necessary, especially after handling raw meat.
2. Use as many fresh ingredients as possible.
3. Don't be a slave to recipes. Modify according to taste and ingredients except when baking.
4. Don't be over ambitious and attempt to run before you can walk.
5. Keep knives sharp.
6. Taste frequently during cooking.
7. Be well organised and clean as you go.
8. Don't feel that you have to be adventurous with ingredients but simply be proud that you can produce a good and tasty meal.
9. Think ahead and if you are able to produce *two meals in one,* do this so that one can be frozen for another time.
10. If possible, avoid eating food straight from the fridge. You will only experience the full flavour if you allow food to warm up a little at room temperature.
11. The best rule of family cooking is to cook one dish for all the family. Meals will certainly become a drudge if you are catering for a number of tastes at one mealtime. Once you step onto this conveyor belt of madness you will be unable to step off.

Cooking with numbers

Metric quantities and measurements are now standard in cookery books but, if you chance upon a recipe from the *dark ages,* most scales will weigh both the old pounds-*lbs* and ounces-*oz* as well as kilos and grams. Also measuring jugs will normally have markings in pints and fluid ounces as well as litres and millilitres. As long as you don't mix the types of measurement and keep to metric or imperial - all should be OK!

SPOONS and CUPS

American, Australian and New Zealand recipes will invariably have measures in spoons and cups. This can cause much confusion as American measures vary from ours and Australian and New Zealand ones are different again! Dry ingredients differ in density and so if weighed by volume such as *by the cup*, they will all come in at a different weight for a cupful. For instance a cupful of flour will be lighter than one of sugar. Here are a few *numbers* which may help.

American Cups

1 cup white sugar	225g
1 cup brown sugar (demerara)	175g
1 cup white flour	150g
1 cup butter/marg.	225g
1 cup raisins/sultanas	200g
1 cup currants	150g
1 cup uncooked rice	200g
1 cup syrup	350g

English Cups

¼ cup	60ml
½ cup	120 ml
¾ cup	180 ml
1 cup	240 ml

English Spoons

teaspoon	5ml
dessertspoon	10ml
tablespoon	15ml

You will see that the English cup measures are only liquid ones. I would suggest measuring dry ingredients up to the corresponding liquid amount on a measuring jug.

OVEN TEMPERATURES

Centigrade	Fan Oven	Gas	
110	90	¼	cool
130	110	½	
140	120	1	
150	130	2	
160	140	3	
180	160	4	moderate
190	170	5	
200	180	6	
220	200	7	hot
230	210	8	
250	230	9	very hot

BAKING AND CAKE TINS - APPROXIMATE MEASUREMENTS

½ cm	=	¼ inch	10 cm	=	4 inches
1 cm	=	½ in	12 cm	=	5 in
2 cm	=	1 in	15 cm	=	6 in
4 cm	=	1½ in	16 cm	=	6½ in
5 cm	=	2 in	18 cm	=	7 in
6 cm	=	2½ in	30 cm	=	12 in
8 cm	=	3 inch	45 cm	=	18 in

Shopping Suggestions

What a chore and waste of time shopping for the necessities of life is! Here are a few ways in which you can make it less of a drag.

SHOPPING ON THE NET

If you have internet access this can be a real godsend especially if you are able to afford buying in bulk all heavy goods and non perishables - cleaning materials, toiletries, groceries, drinks etc. Of course available storage space will have to be considered but think of the time and energy saved.

FRESH FOOD

Ordering fresh food on the internet is not such a good idea and can be shopped for at regular intervals as and when required. If time allows and if it is possible, support your local independent shops. Usually local shops will stock food which has been produced locally and so will be fresher as it will not have travelled long distances.

FARMERS MARKETS

Farmers markets are another good source of locally produced food which normally would not have been reared under intensive conditions and will have been produced within a 30 mile radius.

Good Gear for the Kitchen

If your kitchen is already home to a set of saucepans, a selection of baking tins, frying pans, some sharp knives and assorted cooking utensils, you will manage quite well without needing much more other than a good set of scales and a well marked measuring jug. Buying specific dishes for certain recipes is a waste of money and a certain *bunger up* of cupboards. There are usually alternatives that will do.

When you do need to replace or buy new *gear* it always pays to buy the best quality that you can afford. The more robust it is the more satisfactory it will be for cooking with and easier to keep clean.

CUTTERS, CHOPPERS AND SLICERS

KNIVES

Don't be tempted to buy the cheapest - investing well in some good knives will pay dividends in that they will keep a sharp edge and last for longer. Pick them up to see if they are comfortable in the hand. If short of cash buy cheap knives to start with and then progress later with some better ones. The best knives are made with one piece of steel which runs right through the handle. The handle is then riveted and not glued.

KNIVES - important points.

- Keep knives sharp at all times. Blunt ones, surprisingly, are more dangerous as they are inclined to slip when cutting. Sharpening with a steel is not such a simple thing and as it is essential that you do this frequently I

suggest that the *Chantry* sharpener is ideal as it requires no skill. It has a V shape mechanism consisting of two sprung steels that are set at the correct angle to give both sides of the blade edge the right amount of sharpening. If used a great deal and the steels show signs of wear, the manufacturer will supply spares for you to fit yourself.
- PLEASE, please take great care with sharp knives if you have children. They shouldn't be kept in a drawer but are best placed in a knife block which stands well out of reach from outstretched arms.
- Don't chop or slice on a hard surface as this will blunt the knife. Use wooden or polypropylene boards.
- Sharp knives should not be dropped into a washing-up bowl or sink full of water where you won't see them. Keep them on the side until you are ready to wash them.

Bare necessities:-

1 cook's knife	20cm/8inch blade for chopping, slicing and shredding.
1 small knife	10 cm/4inch blade for general use.
1 bread knife	20cm/8inch serrated blade
1 vegetable peeler	-double bladed, for potatoes, vegetables and fruit.
1 Y peeler	for quick left to right peeling and thin slices of vegetables, fruit, cheese etc.
1 small hand slicer	- *mandolin* - not essential. A simple one bladed affair for thin slices of cucumber, potatoes, fruit etc.
Kitchen scissors	Ideal for snipping *all sorts*-herbs, bacon etc.

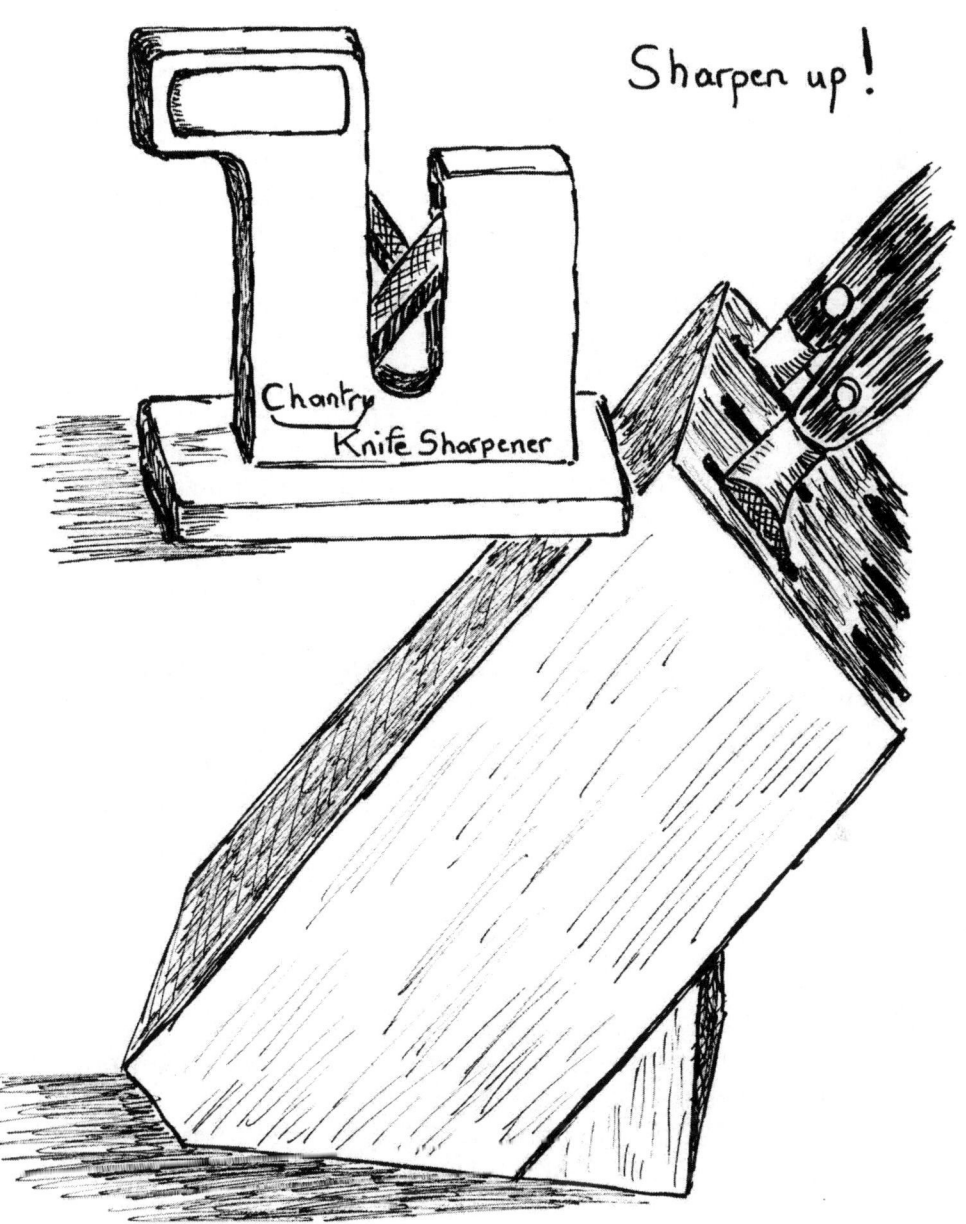

Pots and Pans and Things

SAUCEPANS

Good quality saucepans have a bit of *weight* to them and will be much more satisfactory in use than cheap lightweight ones. A heavy base is essential to ensure even distribution of heat and to prevent sticking and may be even burning! Ideally they should have tight fitting, ovenproof lids and handles that don't get hot and are also ovenproof - this comes in handy for transferring food from the hob to the oven. Most saucepans are either aluminium or stainless steel and probably the stainless steel ones have the most advantages. A set of three in varying sizes should be enough to start with and if of good quality should last a lifetime.

FRYING PANS

One of the non-stick variety is essential and if affordable two would be good. Ensure that the handles are ovenproof so that food started on the hob can be transferred to the oven if needed. A tight fitting lid would he helpful but not essential as if required the pan can be covered with foil or an upturned, heatproof plate. Use with wooden or heat resistant plastic utensils and wash gently without scouring.

CASSEROLES

A large and heavy saucepan would be OK with an ovenproof handle-preferably two handles and a tight fitting lid - also ovenproof. I am saying this because good casseroles are rather expensive but they are the *ideal* for cooking on the hob and in the oven. The best are enamel coated cast iron, two handled and with a close fitting lid. Very heavy but very useful!

ROASTING AND BAKING

Avoid anything that is bendy and flimsy. Roasting tins and baking trays should be sturdy. A medium sized, non-stick roasting tin is useful for many things and especially for producing a family meal without having to sweat over a hot stove.

Electrical Gadgets

My first two purchases would be a food processor and a stick blender. Before graduating to family cooking I would choose a mini food processor which would cover most chopping needs and would be cheap to buy. The stick blender has many uses - top of the list is eradicating lumps in a *gone wrong* sauce or liquidising the ingredients in a cream soup. The longer I have had mine the more uses I have found for it. The latest time saver discovered is chopping the parsley in a white sauce.

THE MICROWAVE - OUR KITCHEN FRIEND

A family recipe book cannot be written without the inclusion of a microwave. For any cook wishing to produce good food in a hurry, the microwave is indispensable for speeding up the process. A recipe which would not be normally regarded as being quick to prepare can be greatly speeded up with the use of a microwave along the way. I have included the microwave in my recipes as I believe that there are very few households without one. On the whole they are not ideal for cooking but good for reheating and defrosting and as I mentioned previously for heating ingredients as you are putting a dish together. Most of us will require only a basic model without oodles of functions. One point to remember is the fact that microwaves have varying power rates - anything from 700w - 1300w. This will mean that cooking times will vary depending on the power of your microwave.

The last time my microwave *uttered it's last ping*, I couldn't delay for more than one day the purchase of a replacement - I am totally lost without one! When buying a new one don't be tempted by the *all singing and all dancing* model. A good make with basic functions will do nicely.

MICROWAVE USES

1. Defrosting.
2. Very handy for reheating a plated meal when, for instance, a member of the family is not present for a meal.
3. Some cooking - especially fish, vegetables and fruit.
4. Making sauces.
5. Heating liquids.
6. Reheating leftovers.

MICROWAVE TIPS

- Don't use any metal or foil (check instructions - this is possible with some microwaves).
- Remember that times of cooking or heating will vary according to the power of the microwave.
- Cooking with a lot of water does not work so well and will probably be quicker on top of the stove.
- Arrange food evenly and not too thickly. Food being heated in bulkier lots should be regularly stirred. This ensures even heating.
- Never put anything in the microwave that is tightly sealed without first piercing the wrapping.
- It is advisable to cook or reheat most food with a covering to prevent spitting and drying out. Covering such as clingfilm should be pierced a few times.
- Food with a skin such as sausages and potatoes should be pricked to avoid *explosions*!
- Be sure to use the defrost power setting to defrost

otherwise the outside of the food will cook before the centre has defrosted.

Keeping Food Cold

REFRIGERATOR - important points:-

- The ideal temperature of a fridge should be between 1 - 4 centigrade. Buy a cheap thermometer to ensure this if possible.
- Keep raw and cooked food separate with ideally the raw food on bottom shelves.
- The bottom of the fridge is generally the coldest. Vegetables and salad ingredients should be kept in the *crisper* drawer.
- Cool hot food quickly and place in the fridge as soon as possible.
- Keep food well covered.
- Open the door as little as possible.
- Don't crowd the fridge as air needs to circulate between the items.
- If possible, leave food to be cooked out of the fridge for awhile so that it comes up to room temperature - but for no longer than 2 hours and keep it covered.
- Don't eat food straight from the fridge as this will not allow you to enjoy it's full flavour. Even salads are best left at room temperature for awhile before being eaten.

FREEZER - important points:-

- Minus 22C is the ideal freezer temperature and should definitely be under minus 18C.
- When freezing something that you have cooked cool it down in the fridge for at least 12 hours. When transferring it to the freezer turn the temperature to *fast freeze* for a couple of hours.
- Food should be wrapped and sealed well with as little air trapped inside as is possible.

- Use strong polythene bags, placed in a plastic container to encourage runny foods to freeze into a *brick* shape. This will save a lot of space.
- Label all that you freeze with what it is, how many it will feed and the date frozen. I have had some *shocking* surprises when defrosting food that has not been labelled. Once food is frozen it is unrecognisable- believe me.
- The longer food is frozen the more it will lose flavour and deteriorate.

THAWING

- Place the frozen meat or fish in a container and place in the fridge or in a cool place. The container will catch any liquid that drains off the food.
- After thawing, make sure that the food is cooked within 24 hours.
- Once frozen food has been thawed, NEVER RE-FREEZE IT!
- If you have cooked the defrosted food it is then possible to re-freeze it say meat that has been made into a casserole, pie etc.

Beat the Bugs

- Wash you hands before handling food and also after handling raw meat and fish.
- Also wash your hands after a visit to the toilet, blowing your nose or touching your face or hair.
- If possible have two chopping boards - a separate one for meat and fish - preparing fish on one side and meat on the other. Use the other for fruit, vegetables etc.
- Keep your knives really clean, washing them between preparing raw and cooked food.
- Don't keep food at room temperature for longer than is necessary. Allow cooked food to only be cooled down sufficiently to beable to place it in the fridge.

- Buy a cheap thermometer for your fridge - the temperature should be between 1C and 4C.
- Place uncooked meat and fish at the bottom of the fridge to prevent it it dripping on other food.
- Keep all food covered in or out of the fridge where it should be protected from insects and airborne bugs.
- It is important to cook food thoroughly, making sure that it is piping hot in the middle.
- When reheating food or warming up leftovers be sure to heat them until thoroughly hot.
- If you don't have a dishwasher - dishes, cutlery and utensils are much better left to drain and air dry after having been washed in hot soapy water and rinsed with clean hot water.
- Drying-up and dishcloths are wonderful *bug gatherers.* If you need to use them, change regularly and wash at a hot temperature.

Tactics with Children

I declare here and now that I in no way pretend to be a trained psychologist but would humbly like to put forward my own ideas on the *theory* of feeding children. I do apologise, at this point, if I come over as being rather dictatorial. I do realise the *battle royal* that parents have on their hands. Food producers and supermarkets are increasingly using their own psychological tactics with parents and children in encouraging them to purchase ready meals and artificial foods that in some cases are not right for inclusion in a healthy diet.

The following will hopefully prove to be a few helpful pointers on food and mealtimes, garnered from my own experience.

- Aim to sit down and eat with your children when at all possible. This can help your children to gain some basic social skills and will prove to be an advantage when

- they need to *make their own way in the world.* Too much finger food is eaten in odd places and cutlery skills are lost!
- Don't ask your children what they would like to eat but make this decision yourself and put it in front of them. This will ensure that you are only producing one dish and not two or three different things! This tactic also prevents them from choosing *junk* food.
- When carrying out the above suggestion you will, at first, most likely have a rebellion on your hands. If they refuse to eat what you have *lovingly* prepared - stand firm, and don't come up with any alternatives. After a few *hiccups* and if they are desperately hungry, your children will eat what you have put on the table. I don't wish to sound like the *mother from hell* but would like to suggest that it does no harm if an occasional meal is missed and I do understand that there will be certain things that your child will simply not eat and so if a certain meal is turned down regularly then you will need to find an alternative.
- Outdoor activities will improve their appetite.
- Try to discourage snacking between meals - this is easily achieved if you don't keep the likes of crisps, sweets, biscuits etc. in the house. I don't mean to sound harsh but the more these sort of things are available and to hand, the more likely they are to be eaten. Try to think of healthier alternatives for those hungry moments between meals.
- Kids in the kitchen! If you have the patience, get your children involved in cooking - they are more likely to eat something that they have cooked. Not only that, most enjoy it and it will help them to cultivate a life-long interest in food and hopefully cooking.

When husband Karl and I owned Ye Olde Welcome Restaurant in East Grinstead I recall tutoring some local scouts towards attaining their cookery badge. My few hours break in the afternoons were exceptionally precious but the excitement generated when these lads concocted their goulash or omelette was something to behold. I provided the ingredients which were gingerly and proudly transported home in their cooked state with a proud reverence. These afternoon interludes gave me just as much pleasure as my eager pupils.

This association led to Karl and myself being invited to judge their annual cooking competition. Camp fires were arranged around a small clearing in a local wood. Two courses were produced - a main course and a pudding. It was as much as we could manage to stifle our giggles and take this all with the sincerity it warranted. Some would attempt something like a casserole which, on a fire, is nigh impossible. The meat would be rather chewy and difficult to swallow. It was a miracle that after these events we didn't suffer from food poisoning.

Cooking for One - Students

The main meals in this book are for 4 persons but accurate measurements are not normally needed for most savoury dishes and it won't be too difficult to adapt some recipes for one. The idea is that you are able to cook yourself a main meal at reasonable cost with the minimum of fuss and without resorting to junk food or takeaways.

Meals based on pasta or Chinese egg noodles are ideal. These two ingredients can form the basis of a nutritious meal with a few added ingredients. The best idea is to keep your repertoire to a minimum. Keep a small stock of the basics so that shopping doesn't become a chore.

I suggest the following for your cupboard. I realize that there isn't a great variety but the basic idea is that you will always be able to rustle up a meal.

Olive oil OR sunflower oil
Pasta - 75g per person
Egg noodles - 1 to 2 *nests* per person
Tinned tuna

Corned beef (or tinned meat of your choice)
Tinned tomatoes
Packet or tinned soup (ideal as a sauce for your pasta)
Tomato ketchup (supermarket own brand is good and cheap)
Soy sauce
Vegetable stock cubes (avoid the ones with monosodium glutamate)
Onions

In the fridge:-

Mature cheddar cheese (more expensive but you need less)
1 head of garlic (a little of this is a good substitute for onion). Keep well wrapped in clingfilm.

TUNA PASTA FOR ONE

2 teasp. oil
1 medium onion - chopped
1 tin (400g) of tomatoes - whole are cheaper
1 crushed clove garlic
1 tabsp. tomato ketchup
75g pasta of you choice
1 tin (approx.200g) tuna
grated or thinly sliced cheddar
salt and pepper

1. In a medium sized saucepan heat the oil and then add the chopped onion. On low heat allow it to cook for five minutes - stirring occasionally.
2. Then add the tomatoes, ketchup and the crushed garlic. No crusher then firstly place the garlic on a chopping board, a saucepan on top of it and then lean heavily on the pan. This will make the garlic easy to peel. Place under the pan again and squash it.
3. Cook on low heat, smashing up the tomatoes if whole.

4. Cook the pasta according to the instructions on the packet and drain the water off.
5. After the sauce has been cooking for a 5 minutes, pull off the heat until the pasta is cooked.
6. When the pasta is ready tip the tuna into the tomato sauce and allow to heat through for 2 minutes
7. Put the pasta with the tuna and sauce and gently mix.
8. Tip out onto an ovenproof plate or dish, sprinkle the cheese over and put under the grill (if you have one) to melt and brown the cheese.
9. If no grill then hopefully a microwave, put the pasta on your plate with the cheese on top and microwave to melt the cheese.

MEATY EGG NOODLES FOR ONE

You might like to keep some suitable tinned meat in your store cupboard for this. If using fresh mince you will probably have to buy it in a pack of 500 grams. In this case divide it into 4 and wrap up the other 3 portions in a polythene bag or clingfilm and freeze away for future use in the freezer if you have one or the ice-box section of the fridge. These can then be defrosted overnight in the fridge or in a microwave just before using.

1 or 2 *nests* of egg noodles (depending on how hungry you are)
1 tabsp. olive oil or sunflower oil
125g mince of your choice
1 medium onion, chopped small
1 clove of garlic
½ cube vegetable stock + 2 tabsp. boiling water
A small quantity of any vegetables, if you would like to add some, but not essential - thinly sliced or in small pieces - mushrooms, peppers, beans, courgette, broccoli etc.
1 tabsp. soy or hoisin sauce

1. Prepare the noodles as instructed on the packet.
2. In a frying pan heat the oil on high heat and then carefully add the mince, spreading it around the pan, and allowing to quickly brown.
3. Lift the meat out of the pan onto a plate, leaving as much oil behind as possible.
4. Put the pan with the oil back on the heat and add the chopped onion. Allow to cook on low heat, stirring occasionally, for about 4 minutes.
5. Add the garlic and cook for 1 minute
6. Crumble the stock into 2 tablespoons of boiling water and add carefully to the pan. Also add the soy or hoisin sauce.
7. If you wish to add any vegetables add them now and cook for a further 3 - 4 minutes, turning them frequently.
8. Finally add the drained noodles with the meat and mix all well allowing to heat through.

Timesaving Tips

- Remove food for cooking from the fridge. Allowing it to come up to room temperature will ensure the correct cooking times and it will also cook more evenly.
- Pre cook or heat things in the microwave before adding to dishes or cooking. An example of this would be when preparing roast vegetables. Different types take different times to cook - most likely you would start with the onions or whatever will take the longest to cook. This heating for 2 or 3 minutes also is helpful when aiming to coat with as little oil as possible.
- Work as tidily as you can, clearing up as you go along.
- A few ready prepared items on standby can prove most useful:-

<u>GRATED CHEESE</u> - A quantity of grated mature cheddar cheese, bagged up and kept in the freezer.

SALAD DRESSINGS - Do more than enough of your favourite dressing for one meal - simply mix in a screw top jar and keep in the fridge.

BREADCRUMBS - made with old bread in a food processor or liquidiser and frozen.

CHOPPED GARLIC - a garlic bargain here or a cheap offering brought home from a holiday allows this very useful standby! When peeling a large quantity, break the heads up into individual cloves and place between 2 chopping boards or something similar. Cover the top with an old cloth and then jump up and down on the top. This eccentric idea will make the peeling of the skin much easier. Finely chop with the aid of a processor if you have one. Heat some olive oil till fairly hot in a saucepan (as much as you think you will need to just cover the garlic) and add all the chopped garlic - removing from the heat immediately - you are not cooking it. Put in warmed, small screw top jars. Store in a cool place.
Alternative method - mix cold oil and garlic together and chop with a stick blender but not too fine. Heat in a suitable container in the microwave till hot but not cooking. Tip into a warm screw top jar and store in a cool place.

STOCK - TO MAKE OR NOT TO MAKE?
There is no contest here -treat yourself to something like a drum of Marigold Swiss Vegetable Bouillon or Kallo stock cubes. If you buy the vegetable variety then this will serve as a multipurpose stock and will be suitable for most things. We are misguided to think that boiling up a pot full of bones is all that is required to make a stock. To obtain the concentration of flavour required, the resultant liquid then needs to be heated until reduced to a ¼ of its volume to obtain a good flavour. I boost the flavour in my cooking quite often with bought vegetable stock cubes and so would recommend that if you use a lot to try and avoid the cubes that contain monosodium glutamate.

WHITE SAUCE - the simple way

For 600ml (approximately 1 pint) of white sauce:-
Measure out 600ml of milk and heat in a saucepan or on high in the microwave until it boils. Soften 35g butter in a bowl and to this add 50g flour, mixing in well with a fork. Add the hot milk to this whisking well and then return to the microwave for 2 minutes on high. Give it another good whisking and return to the microwave for 1 more minute. Finish with another good mixing. If making it in a saucepan pour the hot milk onto the flour and butter and whisk well, return all to the saucepan and replace on heat, whisking till it boils. Cook on low heat for 2 minutes.
Finally add salt and pepper if needed. Cover with a plate to stop a skin forming until needed.

CRUMBLE MIX
This is a handy stand-by for a quick sweet using fresh or tinned fruit in the base of a greased dish, crumble over the top and finished off with a sprinkling of granulated or demerara sugar. For a crumble for 4 persons - 225gm plain flour - grate into this 130gm cold butter and rub the two together with the fingers until of a sandy texture. Stir in 60gm sugar. Make double ready for the next time, bag up and place (labelled) in the freezer.

GREASING BAKING TINS
If doing a lot of cooking a good idea is to have an old jam jar with a little oil in and a decent sized pastry brush or paint brush to grease tins. Do them as lightly as possible.

On Your Marks! - Before You Start

- It helps to read the recipe through before starting.
- Check that you will find all the ingredients easily.
- Most of the recipes - especially for main meals are for 4 persons. If you are one or a twosome it would be a good idea to cook for 4 and freeze the remainder in handy portions.
- Prepare ahead what you can to save that last minute rush.
- Remember to use all metric measurements or all imperial.
- Spoon measurements are specified - level or rounded.
- Egg size is large.
- If using herbs and you only have dried, use half the amount of dried to fresh.
- Preheat the oven if required.

ABBREVIATIONS

g   gram
kg   kilogram
ml   millilitre

teasp. teaspoon
tabsp. tablespoon

MAIN MEALS ARE FOR 4 PERSONS

Soups and Snacks

Ye Olde Welcome Restaurant in East Grinstead was a happy family home for almost 10 years to sons Karl Jnr., Mark, myself and husband Karl. The building was full of character and I would say dated from at least Tudor times. Today it is said that this part of East Grinstead High Street where it is sited (but now a *Chinese*) has the longest run of pre 14th century buildings in England. My domaine was an *outhouse* kind of a kitchen, the condition of which, provided a few battles with the local environmental health officer. Karl was *front of house* and book-keeper. This was our first business after having worked as joint managers for Trust Houses Ltd., running the George and Dragon in Codicote and the White Horse Hotel at Hertingfordbury. With the help of very loyal staff Ye Olde Welcome was a great success. Cheese and Onion Soup was so popular that it remained on the menu for all that time. Mutiny broke out amongst the cutomers if attempts were made to remove it from the menu. The following recipe can be attributed to my Mum as can my cooking talents.

CHEESE AND ONION SOUP

When young, my children preferred me to *blitz* this soup so that the onions couldn't be detected.

1 litre of water
4 medium sized onions roughly chopped
350 grams grated strong cheddar cheese
2 rounded tabsp. cornflour mixed with a little cold water
ground black pepper

1. Boil the water in a kettle and add to a medium sized saucepan on the stove.

2. Add the chopped onions and simmer until the onions are tender.
3. Stir whilst adding the cornflour to thicken it and simmer on low heat for 2 minutes.
4. Stir in the grated cheese and allow to melt. Also add a grinding of black pepper. Don't cook for long after adding the cheese otherwise it will stick to the bottom of the pan.
5. Taste to see if salt is required - probably not as cheese is rather salty! Add more cheese if not cheesy enough.
6. Serve with crusty bread.

GREEN PEA AND BLACK FOREST HAM SOUP

A very tasty soup enlivened by the addition of this German ham, smilar to all other sorts of cured ham but usually considerably cheaper - (Try Aldi or Lidle)

1 tabsp. olive oil
1 medium sized onion finely chopped
450g frozen peas
6 slices of Black Forest Ham
1 litre of hot vegetable stock
1 small tub of low fat crème fraîche (200/300ml)
ground black pepper

1. Heat the oil in a medium sized saucepan and add the chopped onion and 4 slices of the ham - chopped small, allowing this to cook on low heat for 3-4 minutes.
2. Add the hot stock gently.
3. When boiling add the peas and allow to simmer till peas are cooked (2 - 3 minutes).
4. Meanwhile grill or fry the 2 remaining slices of ham until crisp - set aside.
5. Remove the soup from the heat and liquidize with a stick blender if you have one. If not strain the liquid from the peas and mash the peas with a potato masher. Replace the liquid with the peas.

6. Reheat the soup and serve with a blob of crème fraîche in the centre and sprinkled with the crumbled ham.

CREAM OF MUSHROOM SOUP

You will often find *value* packs of mushrooms in the supermarket. Quality will be fine but they will probably be of mixed size or irregular shape. Try to buy ones that are closed or not too far open otherwise the soup will be a rather grey colour!

250g mushrooms
1 tabsp. olive oil
knob of butter (30g)
1 medium onion finely chopped
50g flour
500ml vegetable stock (cube or powdered)
500ml milk
salt and freshly ground black pepper
small carton single cream (150ml)

1. Clean mushrooms with a quick rinse under warm water in a colander.
2. Slice thinly - if large cut in 4 and then thinly slice the other way
3. Place in a large bowl and sprinkle with a little oil.
4. Cover and cook in the microwave on high till tender. Time will vary according to microwave power.
5. Place the butter and oil in a large saucepan and allow to melt over heat and add the finely chopped onions, allow to cook on low heat for about 5 minutes, stirring occasionally.
6. Add the flour to the onion mixture and stir well allowing to cook on very low heat for another 2 minutes.
7. Heat the milk and stock in the microwave till almost boiling and then add a little at a time to the saucepan, stirring well until it re-boils before adding the next amount.

8. Reserve a little of the sliced mushrooms (to add to the finished soup). Tip the remainder, with their cooking liquid, into the soup saucepan.
9. With a stick blender or in a food processor break down the mushrooms to produce a *smooth* soup.
10. Allow to simmer for a couple of minutes, add salt and pepper, taste and finally stir in the cream if wanted and the reserved mushrooms.

CARROT AND ORANGE SOUP

This is a very simple soup to make and a favourite with all the family.

30g butter
1 medium onion - chopped
5 large carrots - peeled and thickly sliced
1 orange - grated zest and juice
1 litre vegetable stock
300ml good quality orange juice
Salt and freshly ground black pepper
300ml crème fraîche
Chopped parsley or chives for garnish

1. In a large saucepan heat the butter and add the chopped onion and stir.
2. Turn the heat down and place a lid on.
3. Allow to cook for 3 minutes, and then add the carrots.
4. Cover the pan and allow to cook for 10 minutes - stirring occasionally.
5. Add the stock, fresh orange juice and zest and cook until the carrots are soft - about 30 minutes.
6. With a hand blender or liquidiser, purée till smooth
7. Return to the heat and add the orange juice and salt and pepper if wanted.
8. Bring the soup back up to heat and stir in the crème fraîche. At this stage do not boil fiercely.
9. Serve with a little sprinkling of chopped parsley or

chives if liked.

JACKET POTATOES

An oven baked jacket potato can make a delicious snack but of course can't be produced in a hurry. The alternative is to cook them in the microwave. Here are the two methods:-

- Oven baked - scrub well, prick in a few places with a pointed knife and place directly on the oven shelf at a temperature of 180C fan, 200C electric or 6 gas. A large sized potato will take about an hour in a pre-heated oven. Test by inserting a pointed knife to see that it is soft all the way to the centre.
- Microwave - scrub well, prick as above and place in the microwave on a double piece of kitchen paper. Cook on high turning half way through cooking. Approximate times will be:- for 1   4-5 minutes
             2   8-10 minutes
             4   15+ minutes

Test if done as above for oven baked.

Topping Suggestions:-

- Chopped bacon and onion fried and browned in a little olive oil, cooled and mixed with low fat crème fraîche.
- Sliced mushrooms and chopped onions cooked in a little butter, placed on potato halves, sprinkled with a good covering of grated cheddar and melted in the microwave or under the grill.
- Flaked tuna, finely chopped spring onion and tinned sweet corn, mixed with low fat crème fraîche that has been mixed with tomato ketchup and a couple of teaspoons of horseradish sauce.
- Low fat mayonnaise with enough tomato ketchup to shade it pink and plus a couple of splashes of Worcester sauce (marie rose or prawn cocktail sauce)

Add prawns and some finely snipped chives or spring onions.
- Savoury mince of any sort.
- Don't forget the baked beans. Heated and topped with grated cheddar and placed under the grill or in the microwave to melt.

FRENCH STICK WITH ROASTED VEGETABLES AND CHEESE

You could prepare a double quantity of vegetables and freeze half away for another time. Also the vegetables can be prepare beforehand and heated in the microwave.

Preheat oven - fan 180C electric 200C or gas 6

1 French stick or ciabatta
2 medium onions
1 clove garlic
1 red or yellow pepper
1 courgette
2 ripe tomatoes
1 tabsp. tomato ketchup
grated mature cheddar
ground black pepper

1. Place a medium sized metal roasting tin in the oven to heat up
2. Peel and cut the onion into largish chunks and place in the microwave on high for 2 minutes. Remove and add a little olive oil and with a large spoon turn over the onions to coat in the oil.
3. Place the onions in the hot tin in the oven and spread out.
4. Wash and prepare the pepper - see illustration page 109. Slice thickly and repeat as with the onion.
5. Peel and finely chop or crush the garlic.
6. Wash and cut the courgette down the centre and then in 2 cm. chunks the other way.

7. Prepare the tomatoes by cutting each into 8 wedges.
8. When the onions and pepper have almost cooked, heat the courgette in the microwave and then as before coat in olive oil.
9. Add the courgette, tomato, garlic and tomato ketchup to the tin in the oven add a little salt and a grinding of black pepper, stir well and place in the oven for a final 15+ minutes or until all is cooked.
10. Halve the bread horizontally and then into portion size pieces.
11. Spread the vegetable mix over.
12. Sprinkle over the grated cheese and grill to melt the cheese.

EASY PEASY BEEFBURGERS also CHEESEBURGERS

It is a good idea with this recipe to double up on quantities and freeze some for next time! Mould them as below and place on a well greased baking tray. Freeze and then lift from the tray and place in a polythene bag.

To make 8
1 medium onion finely chopped
60gm breadcrumbs (if you have no crumbs to hand, weigh the bread, break into small pieces and pour the egg, which has been beaten together with the ketchup, on top and when soaked for a while mash the bread up with a fork)
1 beaten egg
1 rounded tabsp. tomato ketchup
1 crumbled vegetable stock cube or equivalent of powder
500gm minced beef
ground black pepper
8 soft rolls or baps

1. Mix all the ingredients well together.
2. Divide the mix into 8 and mould into burgers, making them fairly flat as they shrink and thicken during

cooking.
3. Place on a greased flat tin and place in the fridge for 30 minutes
4. To cook, give a light sprinkling of salt and heat a little olive oil in a non stick frying pan.
5. With a slice gently lower the burgers in. High heat at first will help to brown them but then turn the heat down so that they cook gently. 3 to 4 minutes on each side should cook them through properly. If you have a lot to cook, brown them on each side in hot fat and then transfer them to a baking tray and finish in a medium oven.
6. The addition of fried onions on top makes them even tastier
7. CHEESEBURGERS - after placing the burger on the ½ roll, add fried onions if liked and then top with slice of cheddar cheese and place under a hot grill to melt.

HAM, MUSHROOM AND CHEESE OMELETTE

No not a frittata and not a tortilla. What do we call eggy creations made in a frying pan in Britain but an omelette.

HAM - Unless one is prepared to pay *through the nose* for ham, what you get is pretty tasteless. For this reason I have been thoroughly converted to tinned ham of all things. It is so flavoursome and relatively free from additives (check on the tin!). Also check that the contents are of prime leg cuts as sometimes they consist of cobbled together offcuts. The tin is usually pear shaped and weighs 454 grams. What you don't use is ideal for sandwiches or can be frozen away for the next time!

You can make your own choice as to what you include in this recipe as long as you use the eggs of course.

1 tabsp. olive oil + 30g butter
2 medium peeled and thinly sliced onions

150g sliced button mushrooms
8 eggs
cooked cold potato cut in chunks (if to hand)
225 gm chopped ham
grated mature cheddar cheese
salt and ground black pepper

1. Heat the oil and butter in large frying pan and put in the onions, stir to coat in the oil.
2. Allow to cook on low heat until lightly brown and soft, turning them every now and again. This could take up to 10 minutes or more
3. Meanwhile cook the mushrooms by placing in the microwave in a suitable bowl with a dribble of olive oil. Cook on high for 3 minutes and check to see of cooked. If not cook a little longer.
4. When the onions are cooked add the chopped ham, stir and allow to cook on low heat for another 3 minutes.
5. Add the potato if using and the mushrooms and mix well.
6. Break the eggs into a bowl and whisk up to mix, adding a little salt and pepper.
7. Add the eggs to the frying pan and stir to distribute the ingredients evenly.
8. Allow to cook over medium heat for about 3 minutes to set the base.
9. If liked sprinkle some grated cheese on top.
10. Place under a hot grill to finish. Be careful if your pan doesn't have an ovenproof handle and don't cook for longer than necessary otherwise it will become rubbery.
11. When cooked, slide onto a warm serving plate and cut into portions. Serve with a dressed salad of mixed green leaves.

MINI MUFFIN PIZZAS

One muffin per person for a snack
1 tin chopped tomatoes (approximately 400gm) or some ready made passata or bottled tomato sauce
2 cloves crushed garlic (or finely chopped)
a small amount of herbs of choice (optional) - chopped fresh basil would go well.
toppings - what you fancy - salami, thinly sliced mushroom, ham, pine nuts, grated cheddar or parmesan cheese, sliced mozzarella, tuna, sweet corn, crumbled ricotta or any crumbly British cheese etc.

1. Make the tomato sauce by combining the tomatoes and garlic in a medium sized saucepan.
2. On medium heat allow to bubble away until reduced by ½ and not too wet. Add a little salt and pepper.
3. Add herbs if wanted and allow to cook for another minute.
4. Halve the muffins horizontally and spread on some of the tomato sauce.
5. Top with your favourites (sliced very thinly) except grated cheese if using.
6. Dribble some olive oil over the top and then grill to cook and heat.
7. Lastly, add grated cheese if using and pop under the grill to melt and brown.

MUM'S CHEESE PUDDING

Preheat oven   180C fan 200C electric or 6 gas

My all time favourite as when younger I wasn't keen on meat but a real fan of cheese. Almost a soufflé but not so refined.

Preheat oven   180C fan 200C electric or 6 gas

150g white bread without the crust
450ml milk
85g butter
1 teasp. made English mustard
170g mature cheddar cheese- grated
little salt and grinding of black pepper
3 eggs - yolks separated from whites

1. Grease a suitable 1.4 litre dish - deep rather than shallow.
2. Bring the milk, with the butter, to the boil in a large basin in the microwave.
3. Break or cut the bread up into small pieces and add to the milk. Stir so that the bread soaks up the milk. Leave for 10 minutes.
4. With a whisk or a stick blender mix the bread and milk to break the bread up - if using a blender don't over do this as it will turn into a starchy puree.
5. Add the cheese, mustard, egg yolks and pepper. Taste a little to check if salty enough because the cheese should make it salt enough. Add some pepper.
6. Mix all together really well.
7. Whisk up the egg white until fairly stiff but not as stiff as for meringues. This is what I call ¾ stiff.
8. Tip the cheese mixture on top of the egg whites and fold gently altogether so that you knock as little air out as possible.
9. Tip the mix into the greased dish and stand this in a larger tin or dish that has warm water in to come ½ way up the pudding dish.
10. Bake for about 40 minutes or until the pudding has set. Keep and eye that it doesn't brown to quickly and lower the heat if necessary.

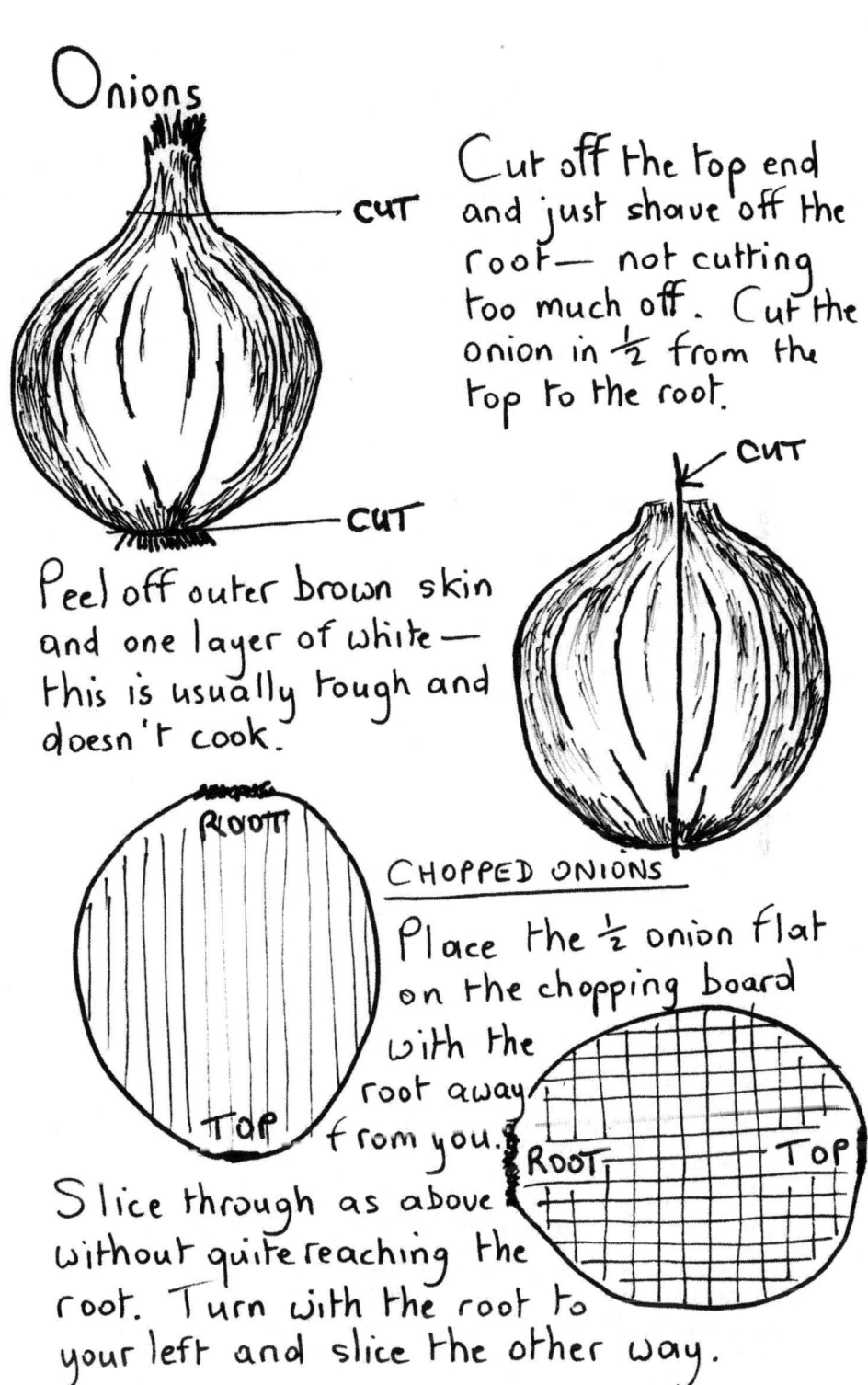

Vegetables, Potatoes, Salads and Dressings.

SPICED RED CABBAGE WITH APPLE

I find this red cabbage is a very handy stand-by to have in the freezer and is popular with all the family. A food processor would be handy for this recipe as there is a lot of chopping and slicing involved.

Preheat oven 180C fan 200C electric or 6 gas.

1 red cabbage (1¼-1½kilos)
3 bramley apples (cookers!) medium to large
3 onions - medium - finely chopped
300ml malt vinegar
150ml water
225gm demerara sugar
3 level teasp. mixed spice
2 level teasp. salt and a good grinding of black pepper or a good sprinkling of white.

1. Peel off the outer leaves of the cabbage and trim off the base of the stalk. With a large sharp knife cut the cabbage in half right down through the centre stalk. Cut each half downwards into wedges - about 6. Either slice thinly in a processor or by hand with a knife.
2. In a large plastic bowl - a clean washing up bowl will do - mix the vinegar, water, sugar, spices, salt and pepper.
3. Peel the apples, cut in 4 down through the stalk and remove the core. Cut each piece into 6 chunks and place in the vinegar liquid, making sure that the apple is coated - this will stop it from turning brown.
4. Place the onion and cabbage in the bowl and with your hands give this all a really good mix around.
5. Divide the mix into 2 casserole dishes with tight fitting lids or 2 baking tins, making sure that there is an equal

amount of liquid in each. If using baking tins cover tightly with foil.
6. Place in the oven and after 45 minutes turn the heat down to 130C fan 150C electric or 2 gas.
7. When the cabbage has been cooking for 1¼ hours remove it from the oven and give it a good stir round.
8. Cover tightly again and return to the oven for another 45 minutes.
9. Remove from the oven and when cool place in the fridge overnight.
10. Bag up, label and freeze.

WINTER ROAST VEGETABLES

This brings out the flavour of the vegetables and is a lot more exciting than simply boiling them. Warming the vegetables in the microwave before cooking them means that the minimum of oil is needed!

1 tablespoon olive or sunflower oil
2 medium sized onions
2 medium sized carrots
1 swede
2 medium sized parsnips
Sprig of fresh thyme or rosemary (optional)
2 cloves finely chopped garlic
½ level teasp. salt and freshly ground black pepper

Preheat oven 180C fan 200C electric or 6 gas

1. Place a large roasting or deep baking tray in the oven to heat up.
2. Peel the vegetables and cut them into evenly sized chunks or wedges.
3. Place the onion, carrot and swede in a large bowl and microwave for about three minutes or until they have thoroughly been warmed up. Drizzle a little olive oil over and stir round thoroughly so that the vegetables

have all been coated in the oil.
4. Tip these vegetables into the hot tin that has been warming in the oven and give a good stir around. They should be in a shallow layer to allow them to brown
5. Place in the oven and bake for 30 minutes.
6. Heat the parsnips in the microwave as before and oil them as before.
7. Remove the vegetables from the oven and add the parsnips, garlic, herbs broken into small pieces (if wanted) and salt and pepper. At this stage if you would like to spice them up a little add a couple of teaspoons of seasoning such as barbeque or Cajun and mix in well.
8. Give all a really good mix and return to the oven for about another 30 minutes (checking after 15 and giving a stir) when all the vegetables should be soft. If during cooking things appear to be browning too quickly, turn down the heat.

MEDITERRANEAN ROAST VEGETABLES

Preheat oven   180C fan   200C electric or 6 gas

2 tabsp. of olive oil
2 medium onions
2 red peppers
1 yellow or orange pepper (not essential, but is colourful)
1 400g tin of plum or chopped tomatoes
1 large aubergine
2 medium courgettes
4 crushed cloves of garlic
herbs of your choice if liked (2 bay leaves, sprigs of
    rosemary or thyme or 1 teaspoon of dried mixed
herbs).
salt and pepper

1. Put a largish roasting tin in the oven to heat up.
2. Peel and roughly chop the onions - not too small.

3. Wash and prepare the peppers as on page 109 and cut into squares - 2cm and add to the onions in a bowl and microwave on high for 3 minutes.
4. Put a tablespoon of olive oil on the warmed vegetables and stir round well to coat with the oil.
5. Tip the onion and peppers into the hot tin and bake for about 30 minutes.
6. Wash the aubergine, top and tail it and cut into dice - 1½ centimetres square - there is no need to peel it. Heat in the microwave for 2 minutes and add to the onions and peppers, again giving a good stir around, adding a little more oil if it looks a little dry. Return to the oven for another 10 minutes.
7. Wash and cut off each end of the courgettes. Cut in 1½cm slices and again warm for 2 minutes in the microwave.
8. Add to the other vegetables, giving a good mix up and dribbling a little extra oil on top.
9. Cook for a further 10 minutes.
10. Remove the vegetables from the oven. Add the garlic, herbs and tinned tomatoes also a sprinkling of salt and a good grinding of black pepper. Mix well
11. Return to the oven for at least another 20 - 30 minutes, ensuring that the vegetables are cooked by pushing a pointed knife into them - if hard, cook for longer

SPICEY POTATO WEDGES

The tip here is to try and use spices or seasoning that you already have. It is pointless to collect a variety of different ones to find that they languish in you cupboard, having only been used once!

Preheat oven 200C fan 220C electric or 7 gas

1 tabsp. olive oil
6 medium sized potatoes

2 cloves chopped garlic (optional)
1 teaspoon of smoked paprika
1 teaspoon BBQ spice, steak seasoning or something of your choice which you may already have.
a little salt

1. Place a large roasting tin in the oven to warm
2. Scrub and clean the potatoes leaving the skin on.
3. Cut into wedges - large chip size.
4. Place in a large bowl and heat in the microwave for 5 minutes.
5. Meanwhile measure your oil out into a mug and mix in all the other ingredients.
6. Dribble this mix over the potatoes and mix well to coat them all. Add a little more olive oil if needed. Sprinkle with a little salt.
7. Tip them out onto the heated tray and spread out so that they are not on top of one another.
8. Bake for 20 - 30 minutes, keeping an eye that they aren't cooking too fast.

FRY-PAN BAKED POTATOES WITH BACON

You need a frying pan for this that has an ovenproof handle.

1 tabsp. of olive oil
2 rashers smoked bacon or a handful of panchetta
4 medium potatoes
2 medium onions
400ml vegetable stock
Freshly ground black pepper

Preheat oven 180C fan 200C or 6 gas

1. Chop the bacon into small pieces.
2. Heat the oil in the frying pan and fry off the bacon until browned. Remove from the heat.

3. Peel the onions and slice thinly.
4. Peel the potatoes and slice thinly, arrange half of them on top of the bacon in the pan.
5. Then spread over the onion and give a good grinding of pepper.
6. Top with the remaining potatoes, overlapping them for the top layer.
7. Pour over the stock and bring to a boil on the stove.
8. Dribble over a little olive oil and place in the oven for 30 minutes. This can also be finished covered on top of the stove but of course the potatoes will not brown on the top!
9. Check to see if the potatoes and onions are cooked. If not return to the oven for a little longer - reducing the heat and if getting too brown cover with a lid or foil.

BAKERS POTATOES

This recipe originates from France and is known as pommes boulangère for the simple reason that villagers would take their dish of prepared potatoes to the local baker to be placed in his bread oven where the potatoes would cook in the residual heat from the baking of the day's bread. If cooking a large meal with lots of dishes to prepare this is ideal as it can be cooking away and then be ready for the final dishing up without any fuss - straight from oven to table!

Preheat oven   180C fan   200C electric   6 gas

2 medium onions thinly sliced
600ml hot vegetable stock (cube or powder)
6 medium sized potatoes peeled and thinly sliced (prepare when everything else is ready so that they don't discolour)
ground black pepper
salt - maybe a little but taste the stock first.

1. In a baking tin about 20cm x 30cm or an ovenproof dish cover the base evenly with half of the sliced potatoes. Give them a light grinding of pepper.
2. Spread the onions evenly on top of this with another grinding of pepper.
3. Place the remaining potatoes on top finishing with a neatly arranged layer (this is only for show so not entirely necessary)
4. Pour over the stock - if it does not reach the top layer add a little water.
5. Over the top dribble some olive oil - this will help it to brown.
6. Place in the oven and bake for about 45 minutes to 1 hour.
7. If browning too quickly - turn the heat down to 130C fan 150C electric or 2 gas.

This dish will keep warm out of the oven for some time but if the rest of your meal is not ready will heat up easily again.

POTATO PARCELS

These can be cooking away in the oven whilst it is on for something else.
For four persons have 4 squares of greased foil ready (about 30cm square). Prepare enough peeled and diced potatoes for 4 people and place in a bowl. To the potatoes add a dribble of olive oil with a little salt and freshly ground black pepper and whatever takes you fancy - chopped garlic, herbs, a little grated or diced cheese, nutmeg etc. Mix all well and divide between the foil squares. Bring the edges of the foil together and turn over to seal. Place on a baking tray and bake at whatever the temperature of the oven is. If the heat is low they will take about 45 minutes.

FILLED JACKET POTATOES

These make a good standby to keep in the freezer so double up the recipe and freeze some away for another time.

4 medium sized potatoes
1 tabsp. olive oil
1 medium onion - finely chopped
2 rashers of smoked back bacon - de-rinded and chopped
115g grated mature cheddar
ground black pepper
olive or sunflower oil to brush the top with

1. Microwave or bake the potatoes as described in the snack section of the book. If doing a large quantity, cooking them in the oven is the best option.
2. Meanwhile heat the oil and on high heat fry the bacon to brown a little.
3. Add the chopped onion and cook for 4 minutes. Set aside until the potatoes are cooked.
4. When the potatoes are cooked allow to cool until you can handle them. Then cut them in half horizontally and scoop out all of the centre into a bowl.
5. Mash or fork over the potato to get rid of the lumps
6. Add the bacon and onion plus the oil that they were cooked in and also add the grated cheese.
7. Mix all together well and place back in the potato skins, flattening the top with a fork to get a rough topping.
8. Paint over the top with oil and return to the oven to heat through and brown.

SALADS

<u>Helpful hints and points to remember.</u>

- Wash your leaves in plenty of cold water but don't leave immersed for too long - 30 minutes should do.
- Drain well or ideally invest in a salad spinner.
- Don't combine too many flavours in the dressing.

- An old screw top jam jar is ideal for mixing the dressing.
- Washed leaves will keep when refrigerated if drained properly and kept in an airtight container.
- If you are making a leafy salad, don't add the dressing until just before serving.
- A large bowl makes *tossing* easier. Ensure that all the leaves are coated with the dressing.
- Tomatoes will go mushy if kept in dressing in the fridge.
- Additions which will add flavour to your salad are, cheese, grilled and crumbled smoked ham, toasted seeds or nuts, a crumbled stock cube etc.
- Serve salads at room temperature and not straight from the fridge.
- With cooked vegetable, rice and pasta salads it is beneficial to add the dressing whilst the ingredients are warm so that some of the dressing is absorbed.
- Don't assume that all salads are cold - some can be served warm.

SALAD DRESSINGS

A salad is not a salad until it has been dressed
Salads are greatly improved and become much more appetising with the addition of a dressing.

MY FAMILY FRIENDLY DRESSING

This dressing is not too harsh and has been a favourite with my family since I can remember. It is particularly good with just lettuce or a green salad.

1 tablespoon of vinegar
2 level teaspoons of caster sugar
2 rounded tablespoon of mayonnaise
a little milk
salt and pepper

1 level tablespoon of finely chopped onion or 2 finely chopped spring onions

1. Place the vinegar and sugar in a bowl and microwave on high for 30 seconds to dissolve the sugar. If not dissolved completely heat some more. Allow to get cold.
2. When the vinegar is cold whisk in the mayonnaise. If this is still fairly thick add a little milk - the dressing should be as thick as single cream (fairly runny).
3. Add the chopped onion, a little salt and a grinding of black pepper.
4. Place in a screw top jar and shake to mix well.
5. When ready to serve your salad add half of the dressing and gently turn your salad leaves until they are all coated. Add more dressing if needed

If you want to make extra to keep in the fridge it is a good idea to boil the milk first. It should keep at least for a week.

FRENCH DRESSING (VINAIGRETTE)

The French would be horrified to think that we've adulterated their famous dressing with sugar but in my opinion it is too sharp without it. In fact any dressing which is too sharp or vinegary is ruinous to the flavour of the salad!

1 rounded teaspoon of French mustard
1 tablespoon of vinegar (white wine vinegar would be best but malt will do)
4 tablespoons of olive oil
1 level teaspoon caster sugar
½ level teaspoon salt
Good grinding of black pepper

1. Place all but the oil in a bowl and whisk lightly together.
2. Gradually add the oil whisking as you go.
3. When all has come together, place in a screw top jar.
4. Before using give the jar a really good shake.

Additions - certain ingredients can be added to this basic French dressing to make it more interesting because let's be honest it is rather boring as it stands:-

Lemon or orange juice can be used instead of vinegar
Chopped herbs - mint, parsley, chives etc.
Crumbled blue cheese - about 50 grams
A little very finely chopped onion
Finely grated parmesan cheese
A crumbled vegetable stock cube - this is a really good idea with a rice, pasta, potato or vegetable salad.

HONEY AND MUSTARD DRESSING

This will go with most salads and is especially good if cold meats are included.

1 tablespoon wine vinegar (malt vinegar will do)
1 tablespoon runny honey
2 rounded teaspoons whole grain mustard
1 clove finely chopped or crushed garlic
¼ level teaspoon salt
good grinding of black pepper
4 tablespoons olive oil

1. Put all the ingredients in a screw top jar and shake vigorously to mix well.
2. Shake well before using.

SALADS

RICE SALAD

1 tabsp. olive oil
340g long grain rice
1½ vegetable stock cubes (or powder) dissolved in 800ml of boiling water
6 slices of smoked Bavarian ham (Aldi or Lidle)
4 tabsp. French dressing
1 tabsp. balsamic vinegar
2 teasp. of runny honey
4 spring onions very finely chopped
4 sticks of celery from the heart - very finely chopped
1 red pepper in small dice
6cm cucumber, halved, de-seeded and sliced thinly

1. Heat the oil in a large saucepan and add the rice, stirring it around so that it all gets coated in the oil.
2. Slowly add the hot stock and bring to the boil whilst stirring.
3. Turn heat as low as possible and place a lid on the pan.
4. Grill the ham till crisp and allow to cool.
5. The rice should be cooked within about 15 minutes and will have absorbed all the liquid. Add a little more liquid if it is dry and isn't cooked.
6. Mix the French dressing with the honey and balsamic vinegar.
7. Allow the rice to cool a little and then add the dressing to it with the spring onions and stir around well.
8. Add all the remaining ingredients plus the ham which should be crumbled between the fingers.
9. Mix all well and chill until required.
10. Toasted nuts would be a nice addition to this - cashews, walnuts or flaked almonds. Add just before serving.

MUM'S TOMATO SALAD

Unless you grow your own or can afford vine tomatoes you will be lucky to buy anything which could vaguely be labelled as tasty. The sugar and vinegar mix in this recipe really brings the tomatoes alive. Make extra dressing and keep in a jar for another time.

6 ripe tomatoes - skinned
4 teasp. of brown sugar
2 tabsp. of vinegar
finely chopped chives, spring onion or ordinary onion
salt and pepper

1. Heat the vinegar and sugar together in the microwave until the sugar has dissolved. Allow to cool.
2. Prepare the tomatoes by skinning them.
3. If possible remove the hard piece at the stalk end with a pointed knife
4. Slice crossways and arrange in a shallow dish.
5. With a teaspoon, gently dribble the cooled vinegar over the tomatoes.
6. Sprinkle a little chopped onion or chives over.
7. Season with a little salt and freshly ground pepper just before serving.

POTATO SALAD

Potatoes cooked in their skins keep their flavour. Either microwave them or place in a casserole with a tight fitting lid and 2cm of water in the bottom and bake in the oven till cooked - preferable alongside a meal that you are baking. You can peel off the skins whilst still warm or if new potatoes I should leave the skin on. I haven't put exact amounts so that you can judge for yourself the quantity that you need.

potatoes scrubbed, pricked and cooked in their skins
onion or spring onion finely chopped
low fat mayonnaise
a little milk
vinegar
salt and freshly ground black pepper

1. Make the dressing in a large bowl. Put in the mayonnaise and add a little vinegar with a little salt and pepper. Whisk well together and then taste. Mayonnaise can be a little bland - this is the reason for adding vinegar, to give it a little *umph*! Add more if you like.
2. If the mayonnaise is still fairly thick - add a little of the milk. Don't make it runny so that it won't coat the potatoes.
3. Add the chopped onion.
4. Dice the potatoes when cold.
5. Finally mix all together gently so that you don't break up the potatoes.
6. A little chopped spring onion or parsley on the top will improve presentation.

COLESLAW

As with the potato salad, I'm not giving exact quantities. A quarter of a white cabbage with two large carrots and one small onion will make more than enough for one meal. A small food processor would be a big help in making this.

white cabbage, carrots and onion
mayonnaise mixture as for potato salad

1. Make up the mayonnaise mixture without salt or pepper - you will need more than you think.
2. Remove the outside layer of cabbage leaves and the stalk.
3. If using ¼ cabbage cut into 2 wedges.

4. Slice the cabbage thinly across the layers
5. Peel the carrots and grate coarsely - to judge the quantity you need as much carrot as you have of cabbage.
6. Finely chop some onion - a little or a lot - to your taste.
7. Mix all together with the mayonnaise.
8. Taste and add some pepper if wanted. Salt will make the coleslaw watery so if you wish to add a little do this just before eating.

Pizza, Pasta, Rice, Savoury Pancakes and Tarts

PIZZA

The base and tomato topping are standard with most pizzas and then you can add your favourites on top of this. Make the tomato sauce topping first as this needs to be cold before spreading on the base or buy a jar of ready made passata, pizza topping or tomato sauce. If this is a little runny, heat in a pan until a little of the moisture boils away and it becomes thicker.

TOMATO SAUCE TOPPING
Buy a jar of tomato pizza topping OR make your own:-
1 tabsp. olive oil
1 medium onion finely chopped
2 crushed or finely chopped cloves of garlic
1 rounded tabsp. of tomato ketchup
1 tin (400g) chopped tomatoes
1 level teasp. caster sugar
1 bay leaf (not essential)
a sprinkling of mixed dried herbs if liked
salt and ground black pepper

BASE
Buy a packet of pizza-base mix OR make your own:-
450g white bread flour (strong)
1 level teasp. salt
1 level teasp. caster sugar
2 tabsp. of olive oil
275ml luke warm water (not really hot and not cold)
1½ rounded teasp. of dried fast action yeast

and FINALLY

A selection of your favourite things to scatter over the top - Slices or blobs of soft cheese, pepperoni, peppers, ham, sweet corn, tuna, prawns, mushrooms and grated cheese or mozzarella for the top. Also a drizzle of olive oil.

TO MAKE TOMATO SAUCE FOR THE TOPPING

Make this first as it needs to be cold for using.

1. Heat the oil in a small sized saucepan.
2. Add the finely chopped onion, stir and reduce to low heat, placing a lid on the pan. Stirring occasionally, cook the onions till soft and not coloured 5-7 minutes.
3. Add the garlic and cook for a further 2 minutes.
4. Add the tomatoes with their juice and bay leaf if using. Bring to the boil, then cook on low heat without a lid, stirring every now and again until a lot of the liquid has evaporated and a thick sauce has resulted.
5. Add the other ingredients.
6. Bring to the boil and then cook for a further 2 minutes, adding a little salt and pepper.
7. Allow to cool before spreading over the pizza dough.

TO MAKE THE BREAD BASE

1. In a large bowl mix together the flour, salt, sugar and yeast.
2. Mix together in another bowl the olive oil and warm water.
3. Pour the liquid in with the flour and mix in well with a fork or your fingers. The mixture needs to be quite moist but not sticky. Add a little more water if stiff or a little more flour if wet!
4. Knead and pummel on the work surface for 5 minutes.
5. If you have a food processor or a mixer with a dough hook this can all be done with that.
6. With a floured rolling pin and lightly floured work surface either shape into one or two rounds or an oblong to fit on a baking tray. Be sure to grease your

baking trays.
7. The dough should be 1 - 1½cm. In thickness.

TO FINISH
Preheat oven 210C fan 230C electric or 8 gas

Children love to help with this part and enjoy choosing their preferred toppings.

1. Spread the cold tomato sauce over the top and within 1cm from the edge - not too thickly.
2. Top this with what you would like, making sure that mushrooms, onion, pepper etc. are sliced very thinly as they have to cook in about 10 - 15 minutes.
3. Put cheese on last this will help to keep it moist.
4. Finally dribble some olive oil over all.
5. If you have taken some time to do the topping the pizza will have risen enough to be cooked but if not allow it to rise a little in a warm place - 30 minutes.
6. Place in the oven.
7. After 5 minutes turn down the heat to 180C fan 200C electric or 6 gas.
8. Another 5 - 10 minutes and it should be cooked.

MACARONI CHEESE WITH HAM

Dry and stodgy are two words which can sum up this dish. To avoid this description it is essential that the sauce is of a runny consistency and that there is plenty of it because as the dish is heated in the oven, the pasta soaks up some of the sauce.

Preheat oven   180C fan 200C electric or 6 gas

225g macaroni - elbow is best but ordinary will do
850ml milk
40g butter
60g flour

2 rounded teasp. made English mustard
½ level teasp. salt
good grinding of black pepper
225g mature cheddar cheese (grated)
175g sliced ham cut in strips

1. Cook the macaroni according to packet instructions.
2. Heat the milk till boiling in the microwave.
3. In a large bowl melt the butter in the microwave (30 seconds) and mix in the flour.
4. Pour half of the milk into the flour and butter and whisk well. Pour on the rest of the milk and whisk again.
5. Replace in the microwave and heat for 2 minutes - remove and whisk well. Add salt, pepper and mustard.
6. Heat for another 1 minute or until the sauce has boiled. Whisk well to ensure that there are no lumps.
7. Reserve enough cheese to sprinkle on top and stir in the rest.
8. Add the ham and pasta and mix altogether gently.
9. Tip into a greased dish and sprinkle with the remaining cheese.
10. Place in the oven for 20 minutes, after which it should have heated through enough.

SMOKED FISH, MUSHROOM AND PASTA BAKE

340g pasta - fusilli(twists) conchigle(shells) farfalle(bows) or similar
450g smoked haddock or cod fillet
225g mushrooms - closed and thinly sliced
150ml milk
1 bunch of spring onions - thinly sliced
1 tabsp. olive oil
1 packet of soup that will make 850ml(1½ pints) - Leek and Potato, Golden Vegetable or similar
1 rounded tabsp. horseradish sauce
2 rounded tabsp. of tomato ketchup

120g grated cheddar cheese (optional) for the top

Preheat oven 180C fan 200C electric or 6 gas

1. Cook the pasta according to the packet instructions.
2. Place the mushrooms and the milk in a microwavable dish and cover with cling film. Make a couple of holes in the top with a pointed knife and heat in the microwave on high for 3 minutes.
3. Place the fish with the mushrooms and milk. Re-cover and microwave for a further 5 minutes.
4. If you do not have a microwave, use the oven placing hot milk in a dish with the mushrooms and fish, covering with foil and cooking for 10 - 15 minutes.
5. In a large saucepan make the soup to the packet instructions, add the Worcester sauce, tomato ketchup and chopped spring onions - stir to mix and leave on low heat for a further 2 minutes.
6. Tip the fish cooking liquid with the mushrooms into the sauce (soup).
7. Break the fish into pieces whilst removing the bones and skin.
8. Gently and thoroughly mix all together - fish, pasta and sauce and tip into a greased baking dish or tin.
9. Sprinkle with grated cheese if wanted and warm through in the oven for 20 - 25 minutes.

ROAST VEGETABLE AND SAUSAGE PASTA

An all in one dish meal - except for the pasta saucepan! If wished serve with a green salad.

225gm elbow macaroni (penne, conchigle etc, will be OK)
2 tablespoons olive oil
4 medium onions - peeled and cut in thin wedges through the centre
3 medium carrots - peeled and cut in 1cm rings

2 courgettes - washed and cut in 1cm rings
450g good quality pork sausages
2 cloves chopped garlic
2 level teasp. spicy seasoning of some sort (BBQ, steak seasoning, spicy season-all etc.)
300 ml hot vegetable stock
2 teasp. Worcester sauce
300ml tub of crème fraîche
115g grated cheddar cheese

Preheat oven   200C fan   220C electric or 7 gas

1. Cook the macaroni as instructed on the packet.
2. Put a large roasting tin in the oven to heat up.
3. Prepare the onions and carrots and place in bowl and heat for 3 minutes in the microwave. Drizzle a little oil over and with a spoon mix well to coat the carrot and onion.
4. Remove the tin from the oven and tip the vegetables (not courgettes) in the hot tin and return to the oven.
5. Prepare the courgettes and cut the sausages into 2cm pieces.
6. When the carrots and onions have been in the oven for 20 minutes, take them out and add the courgettes, garlic, spicy seasoning and a sprinkling of salt - stir around to coat all well with oil. Add a little more oil if needed.
7. Return to the oven for another 15 minutes or until the vegetables are almost cooked.
8. In a bowl warm 1 tablespoon of olive oil in the microwave.
9. Cut the sausages into 2cm pieces and drop into the warmed oil, stir around to coat in the oil.
10. Arrange the sausages on top of the vegetables and return to the oven.
11. Check after 15 - 20 minutes to see if the sausages have browned and the vegetables feel soft when poked with a knife - return to the oven for a short while longer if needed. Cover with foil if needed.

12. Make up the stock with boiling water and add the 2 teaspoons of Worcester sauce to this.
13. When the sausages and vegetables are cooked, remove from the oven and gently pour in the stock.
14. Add the cooked pasta and crème fraîche and mix well spreading evenly over the tin.
15. Sprinkle the cheese on top and return to the oven for 10 minutes to heat through and brown.

CARIBANG (cabbage, rice and bangers!)

A tasty one dish meal made delicious by the addition of a ready-made mushroom sauce or soup.

Preheat oven 180C fan 200C electric or 6 gas

450gm pork sausage meat or 450gm good quality pork sausages.
1 medium sized cabbage - a crinkly savoy would be good
1 tabsp. olive oil
2 medium finely chopped onions
225g long grain rice
salt and pepper
1 jar of mushroom sauce for pasta (about 400gm) or a large tin of mushroom soup
milk to rinse out the sauce bottle - about ½ full
1 vegetable stock cube or equivalent in powder
1 mug water
115gm grated cheddar cheese

1. Lightly grease a large baking tray and breaking the sausage meat into about 16 pieces, flatten a little onto the tray. If using sausages, remove the skin and treat as above.
2. Place in the preheated oven to brown - 10 minutes.
3. Meanwhile, quarter the cabbage down through the stalk, removing the hard centre and slice thinly. Place in cold water to wash.

4. In a large frying pan or saucepan, heat the oil and add the onions and rice and stir well to ensure that the rice is coated with the oil.
5. On highish heat and stirring often, leave the onion and the rice to brown slightly for about 3 minutes.
6. Drain the cabbage and place in the bottom of a large greased casserole or deep baking tin.
7. In the microwave heat the mushroom sauce and the milk used for rinsing the jar or tin.
8. Heat the water and add the stock cube or powder. Mix into the mushroom sauce.
9. Spoon the rice and onion mixture evenly over the cabbage and then place the sausage meat pieces on top.
10. Pour the sauce evenly over the top.
11. Sprinkle with the grated cheese and cover with a lid or foil.
12. Bake for 45 minutes at 170C fan 190 electric or gas 5
13. At this stage remove the covering and check that the Caribang is moist - if not add a little hot water or milk. Also check that the rice and cabbage are cooked.
14. Turn the oven up high and return without a lid to brown the top and finish cooking.

SAUSAGE, BACON AND CHEDDAR RISOTTO

One of Karl's and Mark's favourites. This is in no way an authentic risotto as it can be left to either cook in the oven or on top of the stove and is made with ordinary long grain rice.

450g good quality sausages
50g butter
1 tablespoon olive oil
4 rashers smoked bacon without the rind
1 medium onion - peeled and finely chopped
2 crushed cloves of garlic
250g long grain rice

500ml vegetable stock
Good grinding of black pepper
175g grated mature cheddar cheese

1. Firstly cook the sausages allowing them to brown - either by grilling or frying. Allow them to cool before slicing them into rounds 1cm thick.
2. Melt the butter and oil in a large lidded frying pan or saucepan and brown off the bacon which has been roughly diced into fairly small pieces. When browned, lift out with a slotted spoon leaving the oil behind.
3. Put the chopped onion into the hot oil and cook on medium heat for 3 minutes.
4. Add the garlic and the rice and stir around till all the rice is coated in oil. Allow to cook for 2 minutes stirring.
5. Slowly add the hot stock and pepper and bring to a boil on high heat.
6. Stir and turn the heat down as low as it will go - the liquid should only be just trembling.
7. Put the lid on and leave for 17 minutes. Now check to see if the rice is cooked and has enough liquid. If it needs a few more minutes, add some hot water if it is dry.
8. Finally add the sausage and bacon to heat through for 2 minutes and then stir in the grated cheddar.

PANCAKE PARCELS WITH HAM AND CHEESE

For the pancakes (batter):-
115g plain flour
1 egg
300ml milk
¼ level teasp. salt
sunflower or olive oil for cooking

1. Put the flour, egg, salt and about half the milk altogether in a bowl and whisk together until there are no lumps.

2. Add the remaining milk and mix well.
3. Heat a very little oil in a non stick frying pan. With a good wad of kitchen paper, carefully dip in the oil, distribute the oil over the base of the pan.
4. When the pan is hot pour a little of the mixture into the pan and tipping it from side to side, coat the whole of the base - fairly thinly.
5. After a minute or two turn over to cook on the other side.
6. When cooked, slide onto a plate which has a sheet of greaseproof paper on it.
7. Repeat this till all the mixture is used and placing greaseproof paper between each pancake to prevent them sticking together.

Filling:-

1 250g tub of quark
2 tablespoons chopped chives or 4 very finely chopped spring onions
knob of butter (30g)
115g ham cut into strips (see macaroni cheese recipe for note on ham)
115g mature grated cheddar cheese
115g cooked frozen peas
pepper and a small pinch of salt
30gm fresh breadcrumbs (not essential) and grated cheese for finishing

Preheat the oven to 170C fan 190C electric or 5 gas

1. Put the finely chopped spring onions and butter in a bowl, cover and microwave for 2 minutes in high. Allow to cool.
2. Mix all together with the onions, except the breadcrumbs
3. Lay out the pancakes and divide the mixture between them.
4. Wrap into parcels - fold one side of the pancake over

the mixture and then the other. Fold both ends over to make a small parcel.
5. Arrange on a greased baking tray with the folds underneath.
6. Cover with foil and bake for 15 minutes.
7. Remove the foil, and sprinkle with the breadcrumbs and cheese, return to the oven and allow to brown.

Serve with a tossed green salad.

GRUYERE CHEESE AND HAM TART

1 packet *Saxby's* ready rolled butter puff pastry
½ bunch spring onions - sliced thinly
6 slices black forest ham - sliced into thin strips
250g gruyere cheese - thinly sliced (or buy sliced)
1 large tub (600ml) of low fat crème fraîche
3 eggs
3 large tomatoes, skinned and sliced or some roasted red peppers from a jar
ground black pepper

Preheat oven to 200C fan 220C electric or 7 gas

1. If you can *work* a rolling pin, roll out the pastry a little thinner and lay on a greased baking tray. If not, use the pastry as it comes.
2. Whisk the 3 eggs together, simply to mix them up and with a pastry brush or finger, brush a border round the pastry to about 2cm from the edge. This will colour it nicely when baked.
3. With a sharp pointed knife, cut a line halfway through the pastry about 1½cm from the edge to make the border.
4. With a fork prick over the centre - this will help even cooking.
5. Place the pastry case in the oven and after 10 minutes lower the heat to 160C fan, 180C electric or 4 gas and

cook till lightly golden.
6. Remove from the oven and allow to cool.
7. When the pastry has cooled, press down the centre of the pastry to take the filling.
8. Lay the cheese slices over the base and then sprinkle with the ham and spring onions.
9. Mix together the eggs and the crème fraîche with a little ground black pepper and pour evenly into the case.
10. Decorate with the sliced tomato or strips of roast pepper.
11. Return to the oven for about 25 - 30 minutes at 160C fan, 180C electric or 4 gas.

SIMPLE SAVOURY TART WITH MOZZARELLA or A FILLING OR YOUR CHOICE!

An idea which allows you to adapt to you or your family's favourite foods. A variety of things are suitable to lay on top of the puff pastry and to then be baked. Another alternative to this recipe would be fried sliced onions, 4 slices Black Forest Ham torn into small pieces, roasted red pepper from a jar and crumbly cheese (Wenslydale, Cheshire etc.) over the top. Thin slices of soft cheeses such as Brie and Camembert are also ideal for topping off with.

If you are using anything which you have cooked beforehand allow it to cool before adding to the tart.

Preheat oven   200C fan 220C electric or 7 gas

375g *Saxby's* ready rolled butter puff pastry
1 egg beaten with a little milk
4 spring onions - very finely sliced
250g cherry tomatoes halved
2 small courgettes - washed and very thinly sliced
salt and pepper
200g pack mozzarella.

1. Unroll the pastry and place on a baking sheet. With a pointed knife make and edge by cutting ½ way into the pastry, all the way round, 1¼cm from the edge.
2. Brush the border with egg wash (1 egg beaten with a tablespoon of milk)
3. Bake for 15 - 20 minutes and then leave to cool. Press the centre flat leaving the border to stand up.
4. Place the courgettes and tomatoes in a suitable bowl and microwave on high for 2 minutes. Take a tablespoon of olive oil and dribble over. With a spoon gently turn around to coat all with oil. Allow to cool.
5. Sprinkle the spring onions over the base of the tart.
6. Arrange the tomato and courgette on top.
7. Sprinkle a little salt on and a grinding of black pepper.
8. Slice the mozzarella and arrange over the top.
9. Place in the oven at 180C fan 200C electric or 6 gas for about 20 - 25 minutes.

SPAGHETTI WITH EGG AND BACON SAUCE (Carbonara)

450g spaghetti, linguine or tagliatelle
30g butter
1 tabsp. olive oil
6 rashers smoked back bacon - derinded and chopped roughly.
1 carton (300ml) of single cream
3 eggs
150g grated mature cheddar cheese
ground black pepper

1. Cook the pasta as instructed on the packet and whilst doing this prepare the following.
2. Heat the butter and oil in a frying pan and add the bacon, cooking on medium heat and stirring occasionally until it has browned.
3. Remove the pan from the heat and add the cream.
4. In a medium sized bowl beat the eggs and half of the

cheese together. Add some black pepper.
5. Tip the drained and still hot spaghetti back into the saucepan and add a good knob of butter (30g). Toss the spaghetti with two large spoons to coat with the butter.
6. Add the bacon mix with the cream to the spaghetti, and mix in.
7. Finally add the egg mixture, stirring and tossing until it is well mixed in.
8. Place on low heat and mix well - don't overheat or the eggs will scramble.
9. Serve at once sprinkled with the remaining cheese.

Main Meals - Fish and Meat

FISH

Many children are put off eating fish because of the bones and perhaps have never experienced any other than fish fingers. Many of the recipes use flaked fish which will hopefully guarantee that most of the bones have been removed, taking away a lot of angst and making a dish much more welcoming to the younger members of the family.

BUYING FISH

If buying your fish at the supermarket I would recommend that you buy frozen as it is impossible to guarantee a quick turnover at the fish counter and so you cannot always ensure that the fish is fresh. Frozen fish is dealt with very speedily after it is caught. If you have a local fresh fish shop give that a try. Fresh fish should not smell fishy, have really bright eyes and a glowing skin.

FISH KEDGEREE

This dish should probably be in the *rice section* but as it has all the elements to make a complete meal, if the frozen peas are used, I think it is better included here. It is a dish that is easy for children to eat and which eventually all arrives in one dish.

4 hard boiled eggs - sliced or roughly chopped
450g of smoked haddock or fresh salmon
1 tabsp. olive oil
knob of butter (30g)
1 medium onion peeled and finely chopped
¾ of a mug of long grain rice

2 rounded teaspoons of curry powder or paste
1 vegetable stock cube
1½ mugfuls of boiling water
150g frozen peas (optional)
300ml tub of full fat crème fraîche
possibly a little milk
salt and pepper

1. Defrost the fish if frozen.
2. Wash the fish under cold water.
3. Heat the oil and butter in a large saucepan and add the chopped onion to gently cook and soften for 5 minutes
4. Add the rice to the pan and stir well to coat it all in the oil
5. Add the curry powder or paste and mix in well - cook for a further minute
6. Add a crumbled stock cube and the hot water - stir and bring to the boil.
7. Place a lid on the saucepan and cook over low heat for 5 minutes.
8. After 5 minutes remove the lid and place the fish and the peas (if using) on top of the rice and replace the lid.
9. Cook on low heat for a further 10 minutes after which time the fish and peas should be cooked.
10. With a slice or large spoon, carefully lift the fish out onto a plate.
11. Taste a little of the rice to check that it is cooked. If not add a little liquid and cook for a few more minutes.
12. Remove the skin and bones from the fish and break into pieces.
13. When the rice is cooked, add the crème fraîche, a little salt and a grinding of pepper and mix in well - check that the taste is right.
14. Finally stir in the fish and hard boiled eggs. If the mix appears dry and stiff add enough milk to moisten it.
15. Heat through on low heat, stirring gently.
16. Serve in a warmed dish.

SALMON FISH CAKES

Probably not the right thing to say but there is more flavour in tinned salmon than fresh and as it is being mixed with potato a bit more flavour is an asset. Also tinned salmon does retain it's omega 3 fish oils

1 large tin of salmon (about 420g)
3 medium size potatoes
>   Well scrubbed and cooked (after pricking) in the microwave for about 10 minutes or until a knife easily goes into the centre

1 knob of butter (30g)
6 spring onions chopped finely
200 ml thick white sauce
>   Heat the liquid from the salmon tin, plus some milk to make up to 300ml, in the microwave until boiling. In a bowl mix 30g of soft butter and 30g of flour with a fork. Add the hot milk and whisk - bring back to the boil in the microwave and whisk well. It needs to boil for another minute.

1 egg beaten with 2 tabsp. milk
'dry' breadcrumbs (made from stale bread which has been baked a little in a low oven or put in at the end of baking to harden off a little). It is possible to use fresh crumbs but they do soak up more of the frying oil. Break up the dry bread and whiz in a liquidizer or food processor.

1. Cook the potatoes as stated above
2. Drain the liquid from the tin of salmon into a measuring jug and make up to 200ml with milk.
3. Put the spring onions in a bowl with the butter and microwave for a couple of minutes
4. Make the sauce as above in ingredients list
5. Break the fish up and remove any skin and the large bones.
6. When the potatoes are cooked and cool enough, halve them and scoop out into a container where you can

mash them up with a fork.
7. Mix the sauce and a little salt and pepper into the potatoes.
8. Gently mix in the spring onions and the salmon - trying not to break it up to much.
9. Place, covered in the fridge to cool and set off a little.
10. Divide the mix into 8 and mould into cakes about 1.5 cm thick. If a little fragile, place in the fridge again, on a floured plate, for awhile.
11. If wished at this stage you can fry the fish cakes without bread crumbing them although they won't be quite as crispy.
12. In a shallow dish beat the egg with a couple of tablespoons of milk.
13. Cover both sides of the cakes with the egg and then dip in the crumbs to coat all over.
14. Heat ½ tablespoon of olive oil in a frying pan and when the oil is hot gently lower in the cakes - cooking and browning each side for 2 - 3 minutes. Start them off in hot oil but after you will need to turn down the heat so that they don't burn.

NO FUSS FISH PIE

Fish pie can be time consuming and fiddly but I have made the method as simple as possible. To make it even easier you could do away with the mashed potato and instead top the pie with overlapping slices of previously boiled or baked potatoes, with a topping of grated cheese (as with Cottage Pie-page 81). It is not necessary to cook the fish first as long as you remove any bones and skin.

Preheat oven   180C fan   200C electric or 6 gas

6 medium sized potatoes
4 hardboiled eggs
450g mixed fish fillet (salmon, cod, haddock etc.)
6 spring onions thinly sliced (including the green)

knob of butter (30g)
2 tabsp. tomato ketchup
2 teasp. Worcester sauce
2 teasp. lemon juice
200ml crème fraîche
300ml single cream
salt and pepper

1. Peel and chop the potatoes into evenly sized chunks and put on to cook in boiling salted water.
2. When the potato water is boiling, slowly lower in the eggs to hard boil them (not straight from the fridge otherwise they will crack). Allow the eggs to cook for 8 minutes and the lift them out into cold water.
3. Skin the fish (as in the Salmon en Croute recipe) and pull out any bones - you should feel them if you run your fingers over the fish. Pulling them with tweezers makes it easier.
4. Cut the fish into chunks - 2cm square roughly
5. The potatoes should take about 20 minutes to cook - test with a pointed knife that it goes into the centre easily. Drain the water off and return to a low heat to allow them to dry off for a couple of minutes, shaking them in between to turn them over. Add a little of the single cream and a knob of butter with a grinding of black pepper. Mash and set aside for the topping.
6. Put the knob of butter and spring onions in a largish bowl and microwave on high for 1 minute.
7. Tip the remaining ingredients into a bowl with a pinch of salt and a good grinding of black pepper. Whisk all together to mix well
8. Peel and chop the hard boiled eggs into eight and with the fish and the sauce, tip all in with the spring onions and stir gently to mix.
9. Tip into a suitable greased dish and cover with the mashed potato - forking it over roughly.
10. Place in the oven to brown and heat through - at least for 30 - 40 minutes.

FISH PARCELS

A meal that is fairly stress free. Can be prepared in advance and cooked at the last moment - preferably not straight from the fridge - but if this has to be the case, don't forget that it will take longer to cook.
Any fish which has thick fillets would be suitable for this dish - cod, haddock, salmon or anything of your choice. These individually cooked portions are something different with which to temp children.

Preheat oven 200C fan 220C electric or 7 gas

700g thick fish fillet - boned, skinned and cut into 4 portions. Run your fingers over the fish to feel the bones and remove - pulling or with tweezers
olive oil
spicy or barbeque seasoning (or similar)
12 cherry tomatoes
12 small potatoes with the skin on - well washed
2 small courgettes washed, ends removed and very thinly sliced
1 small tub of full fat crème fraîche
4 spring onions finely sliced
2 rounded teasp. horseradish sauce
2 tabsp. tomato ketchup
salt

1. Firstly, on a flat surface, lay 4 squares of baking foil (about 30cm square) and grease the centre.
2. Chop the potatoes into thin slices and divide between the 4 foil squares.
3. Sprinkle the fish on both sides with the seasoning - be fairly liberal.
4. Heat a little oil in a frying pan till sizzling and quickly fry the fish on both sides to brown - 30 seconds per side
5. Place the fish on top of the potatoes.
6. Add the tomatoes, courgettes and spring onions to the

same frying pan and allow to heat through for 2 - 3 minutes. Divide between the 4 *foils* and sprinkle lightly with a little salt
7. In a bowl mix together the crème fraîche, horseradish sauce and ketchup. Spoon on to the top of the 4 portions.
8. Bring the foil up around the portions, folding over the edges to enclose all.
9. Place on a baking tray and cook for 30 minutes
10. Serve straight onto warmed plates but wait 10 minutes before opening the parcels and be extremely careful doing this.

OVEN BAKED (0NE DISH) FISH

This dish is extremely tasty - if only I could think of a better name for it. As the name implies, the meal is all cooked in one large dish and is really uncomplicated.

Preheat oven 180C fan 200 electric or 6 gas

olive oil
2 medium onions, peeled and cut into 8 wedges - firstly cutting down through the centre and then each ½ into 4
1 red pepper deseeded and cut in large dice
3/4 medium potatoes peeled or well scrubbed, cut in 1.5cm dice
2 courgettes top and tailed, halved down the centre and then in 1.5cm pieces
200g closed mushrooms cut in similar sized chunks to the above
2 cloves crushed garlic
fresh herbs (a sprinkling of chopped rosemary or thyme) OR a teaspoon of mixed dried herbs (not essential)
4 portions of fish in pieces (salmon), fillets (cod, haddock, pollock, whiting etc.) or whole (herring, mackerel, trout, sea bass etc.)

1. Place a large roasting tin in the oven to heat up whilst preparing the onion and red pepper.
2. Put the pepper and onion in a suitable bowl and microwave on high for 2 minutes.
3. Dribble a little olive oil on and stir well so that all is well coated.
4. Remove the tin from the oven and tip the peppers and onion in - spreading out and return to the oven.
5. Repeat with the diced potatoes - microwave 3 minutes, oil and tip in with the onion and pepper and replace in the oven, cooking for 20 minutes.
6. Meanwhile prepare the mushrooms and courgettes and prepare as with the other vegetables but heating in the microwave for 3 minutes.
7. When the other vegetables have been in the oven for 20 minutes add the courgettes and mushrooms, the garlic, a sprinkling of salt and a grinding of black pepper. Mix all together well and spread out evenly.
8. Return to the oven for 15 minutes.
9. Prepare the fish - wash and pat dry on kitchen paper. Brush lightly with olive oil and give a grinding of pepper and sprinkling of salt (not if smoked fish).
10. After the 15 minutes is up place the fish on top of the vegetables and return to the oven for:-
    thin fish fillets 10 minutes,
    thick pieces 15 minutes
    whole fish 20 - 25 minutes
11. After these times all should be ready to dish up.

MEAT

MULTI-PURPOSE SAVOURY MINCE

The beauty of this recipe is that it can be made at any time and then frozen away in batches. It can then be defrosted and forms the basis for many recipes. Also at the end of this recipe you will find the recipe for making one meal's worth of this so that if you haven't any frozen away you will be able to make one of the following recipes that follow on from this:-

Lasagne
Spaghetti Bolognese
Speedy Cottage pie
Stuffed Peppers
Cheats Moussaka
Baked Savoury Pancakes with Cheese Sauce
Quickie Chilli Con Carne

BULK RECIPE FOR MULTI PURPOSE MINCE
(enough for 3 or 4 meals)

This is one recipe where a food processor is very handy for chopping the vegetables.

Preheat oven   220C fan 240C electric or gas 8

BEEF will give the best flavour and will be reasonably priced.
LAMB will give good flavour, but likely to be the most expensive.
PORK will probably be the cheapest but not so tasty.

olive oil
2250g (2¼ kilos) minced meat of your choice

4 vegetable stock cubes
1½ litres or 1500ml boiling water
140gm tin of tomato puree
4 level teasp. of dried mixed herbs
4 tabsp. vinegar
2 rounded tablespoons sugar (brown if possible)
2 tabsp. Worcester sauce
4 large carrots
4 medium onions
salt and pepper
3 rounded tablespoons of cornflour + 150ml water to mix

1. Select 2 large baking tins - roasting tins or any others which have a lip running around them, that will keep any moisture in. Grease the tins and then spread the mince thinly over them. Drizzle the meat with oil. The meat should then go into the oven when it has been heated to the right temperature.
2. In a large plastic bowl (a round washing up bowl kept for food preparation would be ideal) crumble the stock cubes and pour in ½ litre (500ml) of boiling water.
3. To this add the tomato puree, herbs, vinegar, sugar, Worcester sauce, 2 level teaspoons of salt and a good grinding of black pepper or a good sprinkling of white pepper.
4. Finely chop the well washed carrots (peeling not necessary)
5. Peel and chop the onions – if doing them in a food processor, don't do them too finely as they will go watery.
6. Put carrots and onions with the rest of the ingredients and mix everything together
7. By the time you have completed this the meat should be ready – check to see that it has browned and if so remove it from the oven. If it doesn't look ready return it to the oven until it has browned.
8. When the meat is ready remove from the oven

break up a little by prodding with a slice and then tip in with the prepared mix. At this stage, if you wish, pour off any grease which has formed and tip the meat in with the other ingredients. Put a little water on each empty meat tray and loosen all the bits that are stuck to it and add this also
9. Finally add the remaining 1 litre (1000ml) of boiling water and mix all together thoroughly
10. Select two suitable containers – roasting tin, casserole, large saucepan which has ovenproof handles etc. and divide the mixture into 2, making sure that each has an equal amount of liquid. Cover the containers with foil or lids – tightly fitting!!!
11. Place in the oven and leave on the same temperature for 30 minutes and then turn down to Gas 1- Electric 140C – Fan 130C. Cook for a further 1½ hours
12. When the cooking time is up you will need the cornflour mixed with the water
13. Remove the meat from the oven and carefully remove covering or lids. Stir half the cornflour mixture into each lot – mixing well and return to the oven for another 15 minutes with lids or foil on
14. Remove from the oven, take off the lids and allow to cool as quickly as possible. When cold enough place in the fridge.
15. Preferably leave overnight before dividing roughly into 4 lots if a family with two small children or into 3 for a teenage family. One amount could be halved as this amount would be enough for the stuffed pepper recipe which is bulked out with rice. Put mix in freezer bags(check paragraph on freezing) and put in the freezer – don't forget to date and label them!!

SAVOURY MINCE - THE BASIS FOR ONE OF THE FOLLOWING RECIPES IF YOU HAVE NO FROZEN IN RESERVE.

This can either be cooked on low heat on the stove or in the oven. Preheat oven to 200C fan 220C electric or 7 gas if using the oven.

Olive oil
500-650g minced meat - amount depends on family appetites.
1 medium onion skinned and finely chopped
1 large carrot, well cleaned and finely chopped
300ml hot vegetable stock
1 rounded tabsp. tomato puree or 2 of ketchup
1 level teasp dried mixed herbs
1 tabsp. vinegar
2 level teasp. sugar (brown if you have it)
2 teasp. Worcester sauce
1 rounded tabsp. cornflour
little cold water.

1. In a frying pan brown the meat in a little hot oil in 3 or 4 batches. It won't brown if done all in one lot.
2. In between each browning, with a slotted spoon lift the meat out, leaving the oil behind for frying the next lot.
3. Use the same oil to brown the onion and carrot and when ready put with the meat into either a saucepan or suitable dish for the oven.
4. Pour the stock into the (unwashed) frying pan, adding all the other ingredients and allow to heat for 2 minutes. Scrape the base of the pan to incorporate the flavours.
5. Pour in with the meat, adding a grinding of black pepper and ½ teaspoon of salt and mix well.
6. Place a lid on or some tightly fitting foil. On the stove

bring it to a boil and then turn as low as possible and cook for 45 minutes. For the oven method, turn the heat down after 20 minutes to 130C fan 150C electric or 2 gas and cook for 1 hour.
7. Finally thicken with the cornflour by adding it to a little cold water before adding to the mince. Cook for 2 minutes. This can be added to the oven lot, stirred well, and returned to the oven for 5 minutes.

FOLLOWING ARE RECIPES USING 'MULTI-PURPOSE' MINCE

LASAGNE

Preheat oven   170C fan   190C electric or 5 gas

Grease a roasting tin (approx. 20cm x 30cm) or a baking dish of similar size.

1 (defrosted) pack of 'multi-purpose' mince or the savoury mince recipe previous to this.

10 sheets lasagne - pre-cooked variety if possible. I find that even with long cooking the pasta is still hard and so it is best to soften it first by covering with hot water from the tap - this helps it on it's way.
1 400g tin of chopped tomatoes
3 cloves of chopped or crushed garlic
600ml tub of crème fraîche
120g grated cheddar cheese

1. Run hot water into a large bowl or deep dish and place the pasta sheets in separately to soften. If you have the ordinary uncooked pasta - follow the instructions on the packet.
2. Tip the mince into a saucepan, adding the tinned tomatoes and garlic. Place on medium heat and bring

to the boil. Allow to cook on low heat for 5 minutes.
3. Drain the lasagne sheets in a colander.
4. Spread half of the meat mixture evenly over the bottom of the tin or dish
5. Cover this with half of the lasagne sheets.
6. Cover this with the remaining half of the meat sauce.
7. Top with the remaining pasta sheets.
8. Coat the top of the dish with the crème fraîche.
9. Sprinkle with the grated cheese.
10. Place in the oven for 30 - 40 minutes till nicely browned on top and bubbling.
11. It will be much easier to dish out if you leave it to stand for 15-20 minutes.

SPAGHETTI BOLOGNESE

75g (about) spaghetti per person
    cooked as instructions on the packet
1 defrosted pack of 'multi-purpose mince' or a batch of
    savoury mince - the recipe is before the one for
    Lasagne.
200g chopped or thinly sliced mushrooms (optional)
3 cloves crushed or finely chopped garlic
1 400g tin of chopped tomatoes
Grated strong cheddar or parmesan for sprinkling over

1. If using, place the prepared mushrooms in a microwave able bowl and dribble with a little olive oil. Cover, and microwave on high for 1 minute. Remove and stir to distribute the oil. Return to the microwave for a further 2 minutes.
2. Tip the prepared mince into a large sauce pan, adding the other ingredients plus the mushrooms with the cooking juice. Stir well and on medium heat bring up to boiling and then reduce the heat. Stir occasionally and leave to gently bubble away for about 10 minutes.
3. Cook your spaghetti, following the instructions on the packet and allowing about 75g per person.
4. Before serving check the sauce for enough salt and

pepper. To serve, place the spaghetti on the plate with a ladle or two of sauce on top.
5. Sprinkle with the cheese if liked.

SPEEDY COTTAGE PIE

Preheat oven to 180Cfan 200C electric or 6 gas

Tin or dish about 20cm x 20cm - greased

6 medium potatoes (pre-cooked) - with skins on, scrubbed and pricked in a couple of places with a knife tip, placed in a casserole with 3cm water in the base. Put the lid on and bake in the oven for about 1 hour on 180C fan 200c electric or 6 gas. Test with a pointed knife to see if they are cooked through. Before the potatoes have completely cooled, peel the skin off.
1 tabsp. olive oil
1 medium onion roughly chopped
2 carrots, well scrubbed and chopped
2 sticks of celery- finely sliced (not essential)
250g sliced mushrooms (optional)
1 pack of defrosted *multi purpose mince* OR one lot of savoury mince as in recipe before Lasagne.
2 tabsp. tomato ketchup
2 teasp. Worcester sauce
A little grated strong cheddar cheese to sprinkle on top of the sliced potatoes.

1. Hopefully you have prepared your potatoes
2. Heat the oil in a medium sized saucepan and add the onion, carrot and celery. Allow to cook on low heat with a lid on and stirring occasionally. The vegetables will take at least 10 minutes to soften.
3. If using mushrooms, add these to the vegetables and cook for a further 5 minutes.
4. Add the minced meat to the vegetables, adding the Worcester sauce and ketchup.
5. Tip the meat mix into the dish and spread over evenly.

6. Slice the potatoes and arrange to cover the meat, overlapping neatly.
7. Sprinkle with grated cheese and bake for about 25 minutes until the cheese has browned and the meat is bubbling.

STUFFED PEPPERS

Preheat oven   180C fan 200C electric or 6 gas

6-8 peppers (red, yellow or orange)
60g long grain rice - cooked
Small pack of *multipurpose* mince or ½ amount of the recipe before Lasagne
2 cloves garlic - finely chopped or crushed
500ml vegetable stock
2 tabsp. tomato ketchup
2 teasp. Worcester sauce

1. Place a large pan of water on to boil.
2. Wash the peppers and cut the stalks off level with the pepper.
3. Cut in half *round the waist* and remove the seeds as much as is possible.
4. When the water is boiling, drop in the peppers and leave for 2 minutes. Then lift out with a slotted spoon into a roasting dish or tin which is not too large so that the peppers prop each other up.
5. Make up the stock with the hot water and add the ketchup and Worcester sauce - mix well.
6. Mix the mince with the cooked rice and garlic and stuff into the peppers, standing them upright in the dish.
7. Pour the stock into the base of the dish.
8. Drizzle a little olive oil over the top of the peppers and place in the oven.
9. Bake for 30 minutes before turning the heat down to fan 140C electric 160C or gas 3 and cooking for another 30 minutes.
10. Check to see that the peppers are soft - if not bake for

a little longer.

'CHEATS' MOUSSAKA

Traditional moussaka is made with lamb whereas here we are making use of our *multi purpose mince*.

Preheat oven   200C fan   220C electric or 7 gas

1 pack of *multipurpose mince* OR
   a one dish amount as in the recipe before Lasagne.
2 large aubergines or 4 small
olive oil for cooking the aubergine
1 400g tin chopped tomatoes
4 cloves garlic - chopped finely or crushed
600ml tub of crème fraîche or 600ml white sauce(page 22)
100g grated mature cheddar cheese

1. Wash the aubergines and slice off the stalk.
2. Slice them downwards from the stalk to the base - about ¾cm thick
3. Grease a couple of baking trays and spread out the aubergine in a single layer. Brush over with olive oil.
4. Place in the oven to soften - about 10 - 15 minutes. Keep an eye on them so that they don't burn.
5. Meanwhile mix the beef mince with the garlic and chopped tomatoes.
6. Grease a baking tin (20cm x 30cm) and spread ½ of the meat mixture over the base.
7. Then put on a layer of aubergine.
8. Repeat these two layers once more, ending with the aubergine.
9. Spread the crème fraîche or white sauce evenly all over the top and sprinkle on the grated cheese.
10. Place the moussaka in the oven and turn it down to 170C fan   190C electric or 5 gas.
11. Bake for about 40 minutes until bubbling keeping an eye that it is not getting too brown. Turn the heat down if this is the case.

BAKED SAVOURY PANCAKES WITH CHEESE SAUCE

This is a little fiddly but a favourite with children.

Pancakes:- buy ready-made or make your own!
500ml milk
2 eggs
240g plain flour
Pinch of salt

1 pack of multi-purpose mince (with added garlic if wanted)
500ml tub of crème fraîche or 600ml white sauce - recipe page 22
160g grated mature cheddar cheese

Pancakes:- should make 8 and so 2 per person.

1. Sieve the flour and salt together into a bowl.
2. Whisk the eggs and milk together.
3. Make a well in the middle of the flour and pour in about a third of the liquid.
4. With a fork or whisk gradually draw some of the flour into the liquid and mix in well.
5. Repeat this another couple of times by adding the liquid and gradually mixing in the flour until all is well mixed.
6. If you have 2 non-stick frying pans use them both. Place on high heat with a very little oil in. When hot and smoking, remove from the heat, gather together a tight bundle of kitchen towel and distribute the oil all over the pan with it.
7. Replace the pans on the heat, pour on a little of the mix and tip the pan around so that the base is coated - not too thickly. Reduce the heat a little.
8. After a minute one side should be cooked, flip over with a slice and cook for a further minute.
9. Tip out onto a plate. They shouldn't stick together if well cooked but to prevent this you can put pieces of

greaseproof or cling film in between.
10. Preheat oven 180C fan 200C electric or 6 gas.
11. Divide the meat equally between the pancakes, rolling up into *cigars* and laying in a suitable, greased dish.
12. Save a little cheese for the top and add the rest to the crème fraîche or white sauce and mix in.
13. Coat the top of the pancakes with the sauce and sprinkle on the rest of the cheese.
14. Bake the pancakes for 25-30 minutes until bubbling and brown.

'QUICKIE' CHILLI CON CARNE

1 packet defrosted *multipurpose mince* OR a one dish amount as in the recipe before Lasagne.
1 packet of chilli con carne mix
400g tin chopped tomatoes
400g tin kidney beans, drained and rinsed
125ml water

1. Make the chilli mix up according to packet instructions in a large saucepan.
2. Tip into this the mince the tomatoes and kidney beans.
3. Bring to the boil, lowering the heat and stirring occasionally, allow to heat through thoroughly.
4. You may need to thicken this with a little cornflour mixed into cold water
5. Serve with rice - plain boiled or pilaff - recipes follow.
6. Other options than rice are jacket potatoes, tacos, pitta bread or wraps with some chopped salad.

HERE ENDETH THE RECIPES USING MULTIPURPOSE MINCE!!

PLAIN RICE

300g long grain rice
2 litres of water

1 teasp. Salt

1. Boil the water with the salt added.
2. Add the rice and stir till it boils. Turn heat down low, cover with a lid and cook for about 15 minutes or until just soft.
3. Drain in a sieve and rinse under hot water if needed immediately.
4. If for later, rinse under cold water and allow to drain well. The rice can be reheated in the microwave when required by placing in a microwavable serving dish, covering with cling film which has had a couple of holes pierced in it.

PILAF RICE

This rice has a little added flavour and can be finished on the stove or in the oven.

Preheat oven (if using) 130C fan 150C electric or 2 gas

50g butter
1 tablsp. olive oil
1 medium onion finely chopped
300g long grain rice (1¼ mugfuls)
750ml vegetable stock (2½ mugfuls)
ground black pepper

1. In a large saucepan or casserole which can be used in both the oven and on the stove, heat together the butter and the oil.
2. Add the chopped onion and cook on low heat for 2 - 3 minutes.
3. Add the rice and stir around well so that the rice is well coated with the oil.
4. Add the hot vegetable stock and stir till the liquid boils.
5. Add a good grinding of black pepper.
6. Place a lid on the pan and either on very low heat cook

on the stove or place in the oven at 130C fan 150C electric or 2 gas
7. It will take approximately 15 minutes to cook - check it at this time.
8. Squeeze or taste a grain of rice to check that it is not hard in the middle.
9. When cooked, quickly remove the rice to a warmed dish of some sort otherwise it will continue cooking.
10. If the rice has stuck together a little, stir in a knob of butter.

MEAT BALLS IN TOMATO SAUCE WITH SPAGHETTI

olive oil
250g minced beef
250g pork sausage meat
1 egg - beaten
1 medium sized onion finely chopped
2 cloves garlic - finely chopped
60g strong cheddar cheese - grated
1½ cups fresh breadcrumbs
Small pinch dried thyme
Salt and pepper - a little of each

Preheat the oven 210C fan 230C electric 8 gas

1. Mix all the ingredients together.
2. Mould the meat mixture into balls - about 16
3. Place the balls in a greased baking tin (deep and about 20cm x 30cm. Brush them with oil
4. Place in the oven and cook for 10 - 15 minutes to brown.

TOMATO SAUCE
Make this whilst the meat balls are in the oven

30g butter
30g flour

425 millilitres vegetable stock- hot
1x400g tin chopped tomatoes
1 rounded tabsp. tomato puree or 2 tabs. ketchup
2 cloves chopped or crushed garlic
little pepper

1. Melt butter in a suitable largish bowl in the microwave
2. Add the flour to the butter and mix well with a fork
3. Whisk in the hot stock and return to the microwave for 1 minute on high
4. Remove and whisk and return to microwave for another minute
5. Repeat this until the sauce has thickened
6. Add the rest of the ingredients and mix well
7. Return to the microwave and heat until boiled.

TO FINISH

If there is a lot of fat in the tin round the meat balls, after you have browned them, soak it up with kitchen paper. Also they will have probably stuck to the tin so loosen them. Tip the tomato sauce over them and cover the tin with foil. Return to the oven to cook for a further 30 - 40 minutes at fan 170C electric 190 or gas 5.

SPAGHETTI
Allowing about 75 grams per person - cook the spaghetti according to the instructions on the packet - in lots of water!

SAUSAGE PLAIT

This is *fifties* food - 1950's - how I loved it as a child and still do today. My grandchildren enjoy it also - what child does not enjoy a home-made sausage roll and this is simply a larger version with a few tasty additions. If you don't want to fiddle with the plait, simply make it in to a large sausage roll by egg washing the edges and folding the pastry over in half and pressing the edges together. Don't overlap the pastry as it won't rise properly - the edges need to be open.

Preheat oven 180C fan 200C electric or 6 gas

375g pack of Saxby's all butter puff pastry
1 medium onion finely chopped
450g pork sausage meat
1 tabsp. tomato ketchup
2 teasp. Worcester sauce
grinding of black pepper
optional - 4 hard boiled eggs, halved and arranged down the centre of the sausage before wrapping in the pastry.
egg wash - 1 raw egg whisked together with 2 tabsp. of cold milk.

1. Roll out the pastry to approximately 20x30cm and place on a flat baking tray that has been greased.
2. Mix together well all the ingredients except the eggs and place the meat down the centre of the pastry longways and with wet fingers mould roughly into a sausage shape, leaving 3cm at both ends.
3. If you wish to make a plait place the sausage longways in front of you and starting 2 cm away from the meat, take a sharp knife and make sloping slits about 1½cm apart, all the way down each side of the sausage meat.
4. Brush each side edge of the pastry - left and right with egg wash.
5. If you are using hard boiled eggs, push them (halved) into the sausage meat.
6. Fold the top end of the pastry over the meat and then bring the side strips alternately from side to side up over the roll of sausage meat, folding the bottom flap over the meat before you reach the end.
7. Brush the whole with egg wash.
8. Bake for about 40 minutes, checking that the pastry is not browning to quickly. Lower the heat if needed

FAMILY MEAT LOAF

This recipe has been in the family for many years. Sometimes my mother would steam it in a basin and then allow it to cool - we would have it in picnic sandwiches or cold with salad. I prefer to bake it in the oven so that the outside browns. With one loaf, and if your family doesn't have such a large appetite, there should be some remaining for cold.

Preheat oven 200C fan 220C electric or 7 gas
Baking foil and a large roasting tin for cooking

1 vegetable stock cube - crumbled (or powder)
3 eggs
3 tablsp. tomato ketchup
2 teasp. Worcester sauce
60g white breadcrumbs (if no crumbs - alternative at no.2 of the method)
dried mixed herbs - a sprinkling (optional)
450g minced beef
225g pork sausage meat or 4 skinned sausages
110g finely chopped smoked bacon (not essential)
Freshly ground black pepper and only just a sprinkling of salt - especially if you have added bacon.

1. Place the first 4 ingredients in a large bowl and whisk together well.
2. At this stage if you have no crumbs, in this liquid put some broken up bread to soak - this then can be broken down with your fingers or with a whisk after it has softened for a while.
3. Add all of the remaining ingredients and mix well.
4. Place a large piece of baking foil on a flat surface and lightly grease. Cover with more foil to make a double layer and grease well.
5. Tip the meat mixture onto the foil and with the fingers

mould it onto a large sausage shape.
6. Bring the two long edges of the foil together and fold over to seal. Screw the two ends up and pull upwards so that water doesn't get.
7. Place this in a roasting tin.
8. In the bottom of the tin pour some boiling water to a depth of 6 centimetres. During cooking top this water up so that the tin doesn't dry out.
9. Place in the oven and cook for 30 minutes, then turn the heat down to 130 fan 150C electric 2 gas for a further 90 minutes.
10. It is important to let the loaf rest when it comes out of the oven so that it slices well, so leave for 15 - 20 minutes before gently unwrapping and placing on a dish of some sort for slicing with a sharp knife.

QUICK CASSOULET

A delicious blend of meat with beans, garlic and tomato.

Preheat oven 180C fan 200C electric or 6 gas

1 tablsp. olive oil
2 chopped onions
4 rashers smoked bacon - roughly chopped
4 cloves of garlic chopped or crushed
sprigs of thyme or 1 teaspoon mixed dried herbs
60ml vegetable stock
(160ml stock if you have no wine)
100ml white wine
2 tins tomatoes
1 tin butter beans (drained)
1 tin red kidney beans (drained and washed)
3 portions smoked chicken (unsmoked will do)
1 smoked sausage (usually sold in a single loop and in a packet in the cooked meats cabinet)

1. In a casserole that can be used on the top as well as in

the oven, heat the olive oil and add the onions and bacon to brown a little.
2. Add the chopped garlic, thyme, wine and stock and on medium heat allow to reduce in quantity till almost dry.
3. If you are not using wine, at this stage , add 2 tablespoons of vinegar and one of brown sugar - stir.
4. Add the tomatoes and beans and mix well.
5. Finally add the chicken and sausage.
6. Bring to a boil.
7. Cover with a lid or foil and place in the oven.
8. Turn the oven down to 130C fan 150C electric or 2 gas
9. Cook for 45 minutes and then remove the lid for the last 15 minutes.
10. To serve divide the chicken and sausage into 4 portions.

PORK AND BARLEY BAKE

Pork shoulder is often sold cheaper than other cuts in the supermarket. It may be rolled up as a roasting joint. If you have a sharp knife it is not too difficult to cut up. If there is too much freeze it for later or cook double the quantity and freeze half.

Preheat oven   180C fan 200C electric or 6 gas

675gm diced pork (2cm square)
1 tabsp. olive oil
2 chopped onions
2 carrots in 2cm pieces
2 sticks celery in 2cm pieces
1 can strong cider (440ml)
400ml of vegetable stock
1 tabsp. Worcester sauce
ground black pepper
170gm pearl barley

1. In a casserole that can be used on the top as well as in the oven heat the olive oil. Start off with a frying pan if

you haven't a suitable casserole.
2. On high heat brown the meat - putting about a quarter in at a time, removing with a slotted spoon and reserving.
3. In the same pan brown the onion a little and then add the rest of the vegetables and allow to brown a little also.
4. Place the meat with the vegetables and add the cider, stock and Worcester sauce and a good grinding of pepper.
5. Bring to the boil, add the pearl barley and stir to mix.
6. Return to a boil.
7. Cover and place in the oven, but after 10 minutes turn the temperature down to 100C fan 120C electric or ½ gas and cook for 3 hours

EVERYDAY BEEF (OR PORK) CASSEROLE

sunflower or olive oil
750g diced (2cm square) braising steak or shoulder of pork
2 medium onions skinned and diced
2 medium carrots peeled and thickly sliced
2 rounded tablespoons flour
1 can (440ml) strong beer
vegetable stock to top up
sprinkling of dried mixed herbs
2 tabsp. tomato ketchup
2 teasp. Worcester sauce
1 level tablespoon sugar (brown if you have it)
200g thickly sliced mushrooms (optional)

Preheat oven   180C fan 200 electric or 6 gas

A casserole that goes on the hob and in the oven is ideal – if not brown the meat in a fry pan and then transfer to a lidded pot or casserole.

1. Heat a little oil in the casserole or fry pan and brown the meat in 3 or 4 lots, lifting it out with a slotted spoon – so that the oil is left to fry the next lot.
2. Add a little more oil to the pan and brown the onion and carrots.
3. Sprinkle the flour on top of the onions and carrots and stir in, allowing to heat through on low heat for 2 minutes
4. To this then add half the beer very gently stirring it in well
5. Add the remaining ingredients, except the meat, and stir in well.
6. Add the meat and if there is not enough liquid to cover, add enough vegetable stock to do so – mix well. Bring to a boil.
7. Cover with a lid and place in the oven.
8. After 10 minutes reduce the heat to 100C fan 120C electric or ½ gas.
9. Cook for 3 hrs.

BASIC CHICKEN CURRY

2 tabsp. olive oil
3 to 4 chicken breasts (approximately 700g)
2 medium onions - chopped small
2 chopped cloves of garlic
2 level tabsp.of hot (Madras) curry powder
½ teasp. ground ginger
½ teasp. ground cinnamon
1 rounded tabsp. flour
370ml hot vegetable stock
2 rounded tabsp. tomato ketchup
2 rounded tabsp. mango chutney or HP sauce (optional)
2 dessert apples (optional)
50g sultanas or raisins (optional)
salt to taste
6 tabsp. plain yoghurt

1. Cut the chicken into largish cubes.
2. Heat one tablespoon of oil in a frying pan and quickly brown the chicken - not too much at a time - probably in three lots.
3. With a slotted spoon drain the oil from the chicken and reserve the meat on a plate.
4. Adding the remaining tablespoon of oil, heat and add the onions. Allow to cook on medium gas for about 5 minutes.
5. Add the garlic, curry powder, cinnamon and ginger and mix well.
6. Cook on low heat for 2 minutes and then add the flour and stir in. Cook for a further minute.
7. Add a little of the hot stock with the tomato ketchup, (chutney or HP Sauce if using) and mix well allowing to bubble.
8. Add the remaining stock a little at a time, mixing well in between.
9. When all the stock has been added, allow to cook on low heat for 10 minutes - stirring occasionally.
10. If liked add the peeled and cored apple at this stage and the sultanas.
11. Finally drop in the chicken and cook on low heat for 10 minutes.
12. To finish, stir in the yoghurt.

SAUSAGE AND ONION BATTER (TOAD IN THE HOLE)

Preheat oven 200C fan 220C electric or 7 gas

Roasting tin about 30cm x 20cm
1 tabsp. olive oil
2 medium sized onions - thinly sliced
450gm good pork sausages - brushed with oil
2 rashers smoked back bacon - chopped roughly

For the batter -
115gm plain flour
Pinch of salt
2 eggs
280ml milk

1. Put the oil in a roasting tin and place in the oven for 5 minutes to warm.
2. Thinly slice the onion and place in the hot tin, turning around well to coat the onions in oil.
3. Sprinkle the bacon over.
4. Place the oiled sausages on top and return to the oven for 10 minutes.
5. Make the batter by placing the flour and salt in a bowl.
6. In another bowl whisk the milk and eggs together.
7. In the centre of the flour make a hole and pour in ½ of the liquid and with a whisk gradually bring some of the flour in.
8. Pour the remaining liquid in and gradually bring the remaining flour in so that all is well mixed together.
9. When the sausages have been in the oven for 10 minutes gently pour the batter around them and return to the oven for 25 - 30 minutes.
10. Make sauce if required.

QUICK SAUCE
Make a quick sauce with a packet of French onion soup, adding a good dash of tomato ketchup, Worcester sauce and a rounded teaspoon of ready made mustard.

MINTY LAMB HOT POT

A sort of Lancashire Hot Pot with variations - but cooked fairly slowly it is a delicious combination of flavours and is almost a complete meal except for a vegetable of some sort.

Preheat oven 200C fan 22OC electric or 7 gas

550ml vegetable stock
¾ of 200gm jar of mint jelly
1 tabsp. vinegar
2 level teasp. sugar (brown if you have it)
2 medium onions finely sliced
4-6 peeled medium potatoes
4 best end neck of lamb chops or 4 portions of lamb
(ordinary chops or steaks)
little salt and a good grinding of black pepper
olive oil

1. Firstly ensure that you have the onions ready sliced.
2. Make the vegetable stock with boiling water and add the mint jelly, sugar and vinegar. Stir to mix well.
3. In a deep ovenproof dish (just large enough for a single layer of the meat) place a layer of thinly sliced potatoes (half of what you intend to use).
4. Evenly spread half of the sliced onions over the potato.
5. Pour in the stock mix.
6. Layer the lamb over.
7. Sprinkle over the salt and pepper.
8. Lay the remaining sliced onion over the lamb and the remainder of the potatoes - thinly sliced. The top layer of potatoes make the dish attractive if arranged neatly overlapping.
9. If the liquid does not come up to just under the top layer of potatoe - add some water to do this.
10. Dribble some olive oil over the top.
11. Cover, either with a lid or some foil.
12. Place in the oven and after ½ hour turn down to 100C fan 120C electric or ½ gas and cook for at least another 2 hours.
13. Take out of the oven and remove the covering and return to the oven to cook for a further ½ hour to brown the top.

CORNED BEEF HASH with FRIED EGGS

When you are boiling or baking potatoes do some extra ready for this dish. The addition of cheese, which melts within the mix, is a delicious extra.

2 medium sized peeled and thinly sliced onions
30g butter
1 tabsp. olive oil
4-6 medium cold and peeled and pre-cooked (boiled) potatoes, diced - about 1.5 cm square
a little salt and a grinding of black pepper
1 340g tin corned beef (best if been in fridge for 24 hours) cut in 1cm dice
300ml vegetable stock
175g cheddar cheese
4 eggs

1. Heat the olive oil and butter in a large frying pan and add the onions. Over medium heat allow to fry and colour a little, stirring and turning as needed.
2. When the onions are almost cooked add the potatoes, allowing these to brown and warm through.
3. If your frying pan is not large enough, divide this mixture between two. If this is not possible turn the oven on high and finish the recipe in a large roasting tin.
4. When the potatoes have browned add the corned beef and the cheese if using.
5. Gently mix all and allow to heat through - turning over once or twice. Add a little salt and a grinding of black pepper.
6. By now the mixture may be a little dry so add a little stock if liked.
7. Fry the eggs and serve on top.

SWEET AND SOUR PORK

This dish can be cooked on the stove or in the oven. If oven cooking preheat it to 180C fan 200C electric or 6 gas.

olive oil
750g diced pork (shoulder would be good)
1 tabsp. olive oil for browning meat
1 tabsp. olive oil for making sauce
1 medium peeled and chopped onion
1 red pepper deseeded and diced
1 green pepper deseeded and diced
2 cloves chopped garlic
1 small tin pineapple rings
550ml vegetable stock
4 tabsp. tomato ketchup
1 tabsp. vinegar
1 level tabsp. brown sugar
2 level tabsp. cornflour
2 tabsp. water

1. Heat one tablespoon of oil in a largish saucepan or an ovenproof casserole that can be used on the stove and fry off the chopped onion and diced peppers gently for about 5 minutes.
2. Add the garlic, juice from the pineapple, stock, ketchup, vinegar and brown sugar and bring to a gentle boil. Add salt and pepper as needed, tasting at this stage to see if you like it. Make additions to it if you don't - more sugar for the sweet and more vinegar for the sour.
3. Thicken the sauce by mixing the cornflour with 2 tablespoons of cold water, adding this to the boiling liquid and stirring well. Set aside on a low heat
4. Heat the other oil in a frying pan and in about 3 batches fry off the pork very quickly to brown it, over high heat, lifting the browned pork with a slotted spoon into the sauce, hopefully leaving enough oil behind to

brown the rest. After frying the final batch, ladle a little of the sauce liquid into the frying pan and put on the heat to rinse out the residue - tip it back into the sauce.
5. Make sure that the liquid comes to the top of the meat and if it doesn't, top it up with water.
6. Allow all to come to the boil and if you're cooking it in a saucepan on top of the stove, turn the heat down as low as possible - it should hardly be boiling - in fact only trembling. Place a lid on and cook for 2½ hours - stirring occasionally.
7. If cooking in the oven, allow to come to boil, place a lid on and place in the oven for 2½ - 3 hours, turning the temperature down to 100C fan 120C electric or ½ gas
8. Finally add the pineapple cut into smallish pieces.
9. Serve with noodles or rice - medium egg noodles would be the quickest and easiest.

SPRING ROLLS WITH DIPPING SAUCE

Normally these would be deep fried but we're going for the option of baking them in the oven. Unfortunately *calorifically* there will not be much difference as we will need a fair amount of butter with which to grease the sheets of pastry.

olive oil
450g minced pork
1 medium onion - skinned and finely chopped
1 medium leek- washed and sliced finely- if the green part seems tough don't use it.
bean sprouts - a handful (optional)
2 cloves chopped garlic
4 teasp. soy sauce (or Worcester sauce)
1 tabsp. sherry (not essential)
2 tabsp. tomato ketchup
freshly ground black pepper
packet of filo pastry

butter and olive oil to brush the filo with (start by melting 30g butter with one tablespoon of oil in the microwave - do more when needed)

Preheat oven   180C fan   200 electric or 6 gas

1. The filling will need to be cold before wrapping in the pastry so we will start with this.
2. Heat a little olive oil in a frying pan and dividing the pork into 2 lots, fry it quickly to brown a little. When done remove with a slotted spoon and reserve, leaving the oil behind.
3. To the same pan add the chopped onion and gently fry for 3 minutes and then add the leek and garlic, stirring occasionally for another 5 minutes or until they are almost cooked. If using bean sprouts add these near the end of cooking.
4. Add the pork back into the pan and mix well together, adding the soy sauce, sherry and tomato ketchup.
5. Add a good grinding of black pepper.
6. Cook a little more to evaporate some of the liquid.
7. Check whether any salt is needed.
8. Allow to cool before wrapping in the filo pastry
9. When you remove the pastry from the packet keep it under a damp cloth (tea towel) to prevent it from drying out.
10. Each roll should have at least 2 thicknesses of pastry so cut each sheet in half, buttering and oiling each piece before laying on top of each other.
11. Place a portion of filling at one end and roll up bringing the sides in before reaching the end - making an enclosed roll (parcel).
12. Place on a greased baking tray and brush each one with the melted butter/oil mix.
13. Bake for 25 minutes.
14. Serve with dipping sauce

DIPPING SAUCE

1 tabsp. cornfour
4 tabsp. cold water
1 tabsp. tomato puree
2 tabsp. vinegar
2 tabsp. orange juice (from 1 orange)
2 tabsp. soy sauce
2 level tabsp. sugar (brown if you have it)
2 teasp. olive oil or 30g butter

1. In a small saucepan mix the water and cornflour till smooth.
2. Add the remaining ingredients and stir over medium heat until the sauce thickens and comes to the boil.
3. Cook on low heat for a further 2 minutes.

CRISPY CHICKEN WITH TOMATO DIP

A popular *finger licking* meal with children, making it ideal to serve with baked potato wedges that can also be dipped. Try serving with some strips of raw vegetables that would be suitable for dipping - carrot, celery, cucumber, spring onion, pepper etc. Alternatively serve with a green salad.

Preheat oven 200C fan 220C electric or 7 gas

2 large chicken breasts
115g white bread crumbs
60g finely grated mature cheddar
small pinch of chilli powder (optional)
grinding of black pepper
1 tabsp. sunflower oil

1. Mix the crumbs , cheese and chilli powder in a shallow dish.
2. Oil a baking tray, large enough to take the chicken in a

single layer.
3. Cut the chicken into strips, not too fine, and keeping them near enough to the same thickness.
4. Firstly they need to be coated in oil so in a large bowl warm a tablespoon of oil for about 30 seconds. Warm oil will coat easier. Drop in the chicken strips and mix around to coat them all with oil.
5. Then one at a time drop into the crumb mix and press on the crumbs.
6. Remove to the baking tray so that they are not touching one another and dribble a little oil over.
7. Put in the oven for 15 minutes within which time they should be crispy and brown. Remove to a plate with kitchen towel on to soak up any extra fat.

DIPPING SAUCE

2 spring onions finely chopped (or half an ordinary onion)
2 teasp. olive oil
Pinch of chilli powder (very little)
6 tabsp. tomato ketchup
2 teasp. Worcester sauce
4 tabsp. fresh orange juice

1. Heat the olive oil in a small saucepan and add the onion and chilli powder.
2. Allow to cook on low heat - 1 minute for spring onions and 3 for ordinary onion.
3. Add the remaining ingredients and mix well.
4. Bring to the boil and then cook on low heat for about eight minutes.

ROAST CHICKEN with GRAVY and ROAST POTATOES

This sounds like half a meal and it is. I would like to tell you my method for making gravy as it is so simple and for producing crispy roast potatoes. The gravy can be adapted to all types of roast meat. To complete the meal you will obviously add your choice of vegetables and any accompaniments to the chicken that you might like - rashers of smoked bacon, chipolata sausages, parsley and thyme stuffing or bread sauce. I am a fan of slow cooking although a chicken of the size below can be cooked in 1 hour 20 minutes at a fairly high temperature! A slower method produces meat which is tender and will fall off the bone.

ROAST CHICKEN

Preheat oven 200C fan 220C electric or 7 gas

1¼ - 1½ kilo chicken (enough for 4 persons) A larger one would allow for another meal.
olive oil
salt and pepper

1. Oil the bird all over, rubbing it on with your hands and place on its back in a roasting tin.
2. Lightly sprinkle with salt and a good grinding of black pepper.
3. Pour boiling water into the bottom of the tin to a depth of 4cm.
4. Place in the preheated oven and leave to brown for 20 minutes in a fan oven and for 30 minutes in others.
5. Remove from the oven and cover in a tent of foil wrapping it under the edge of the tin.
6. Return to the oven and reduce the heat to 130C fan 150C electric or 2 gas. Cook for at least another 2 hours.
7. The test to see if the chicken is cooked is to drive something pointed into the thickest part - the thigh, and if the juice is clear the bird is done.
8. **MOST IMPORTANT - allow the chicken to stand for at least 20 minutes, covered with the foil to keep it warm.** It will be much easier to carve. The same goes for all roast meat.

BIGGER BIRDS Cook for up to 3 hours but if a lot bigger you will need to cook it at a higher temperature for instance 140C fan 160 electric or 3 gas for a bird that is ½ kilo heavier and for one that is 1 kilo heavier - 160C fan 180 electric or 4 gas.

GRAVY

1. Tip all but a little of the juices from the roasting tin into a glass or 'see through' jug or basin and allow to stand.
2. Return the roasting tin to the oven for a few minutes where it will brown the sediment left in the tin - keep an eye on it so it doesn't burn.
3. Skim off as much fat as you can from the top of the juices that you poured from the roasting tin and if you feel that you would like more gravy add some vegetable stock or vegetable cooking water.
4. Heat this in the microwave till boiling.
5. Mix one level tablespoon of cornflour with a little cold water (enough for 550ml) and slowly whisk into the heated liquid.
6. When the residue in the tin has browned add the heated liquid to the roasting tin and mix in well.
7. Return the tin to the oven for 5 minutes where it will thicken.
8. If wished, you can strain the gravy but it isn't necessary.
9. Taste to see if there is sufficient salt and add a little ground pepper.

ROAST POTATOES

1. Place a suitable sized roasting tin in a hot oven (200C fan 220C electric or 7 gas) with 2 tablespoons of sunflower oil - shouldn't be in there for longer that 5 - 10 minutes.
2. Peel the required amount of potatoes and cut into a regular size.
3. Bring to the boil in salted water and cook for 5 minutes.

4. Drain in a colander and return to the saucepan on low heat and allow them to dry out for a couple of minutes, shaking them around so that the outside gets roughened up.
5. Tip them gently into the tin of heated oil and with a slice gently move them around to coat them in the oil.
6. Place the potatoes in the hot oven. You will need to turn the heat down a little after a while. It helps to turn them at least once during cooking. They will take 30 - 40 minutes to cook.

Food for Friends

An important point to remember when entertaining family or friends is not to be away in the kitchen for longer than is necessary. If doing a 3 course meal it is always a good idea to choose a cold starter and sweet. Prepare as much as is possible beforehand. Most of the following recipes will not be difficult to finish off at the last minute

BEEF STROGANOFF

A dish which was fashionable in the 1960's but one which is tasty and a little different from the norm. There is no reason why we shouldn't bring back some of the old tried and tested recipes. There has been much discussion as to what the authentic and original ingredients were when this was cooked for the Russian family Stroganov - this is of no relevance as long as the resultant dish is acceptable. Traditionally it is served with rice but is also good with pasta. Don't leave all the cooking until visitors arrive.

To do beforehand:-
Cook the rice and refrigerate (pages 85/86). Microwave when required.
Do no's 1 to 6 of the recipe but keep the meat and sauce separately in the fridge.
To serve - heat the sauce and do as number 7

500g fillet steak (if too expensive try rump or sirloin steak)

Ask for the thin ends of the fillet which should be a lot cheaper than the thicker end used for fillet steaks. It's probably a good idea to order them from the butcher beforehand so that he has a chance to save them for you.

1 tabsp. olive oil
1 good knob of butter (30g)

1 medium onion finely chopped
150g finely sliced button mushrooms
½ vegetable stock cube with 300ml hot water
1 small tub crème fraîche   (300ml)
1 rounded teasp. cornflour dissolved in 1 tabsp. water
½ cup of sherry or white wine or 3 tablespoons of brandy

1. It is very important to cut the meat properly so that it doesn't appear chewy. If you have purchased fillet steak and hopefully bought it in one piece, you will notice that the grain of the meat runs from one end to the other where the butcher has cut it from the bigger piece for you. Cut 1cm thick round slices from it and then each slice into strips 1cm wide. If you have purchased rump or sirloin steaks and they are on the thick side you will need to cut each strip that you cut, into ½ again. The idea, whatever cut of meat you have, is to cut across the grain and not with it.
2. Heat the oil and butter together in a large frying pan. When really hot gently lower some beef strips into the fat - not putting too many in at one time and allowing them to brown very quickly - turning them once. 500gm weight of meat will need to be done in two lots. Lift the meat out with a slotted spoon onto a plate, reserving the fat in the pan.
3. Into the hot fat put the onions and fry on low heat, stirring every now and again.
4. After 5 minutes add the mushrooms and allow to cook, turning occasionally, for another 8 minutes or until all are soft. Add more oil if they become too dry.
5. Add the stock and cook for a further 5 minutes.
6. Mix the cornflour and water and add to the pan, stirring well. Allow to come back to a boil and then leave on low heat for 2 minutes.
7. Add the alcohol and the crème fraîche and stir in well.
8. When the sauce is hot add the strips of meat with any juice that is on the plate and stir in. Allow to warm through on low heat for a further 2 minutes. Add a little salt and a good grinding of black pepper - taste.

Peppers

Wash and dry.
Stand the pepper on it's base and hold onto the stalk firmly.
For stuffed pepper — halve from stalk to base or around middle. Remove seeds.

CUT

For chopped and sliced — with about 4 curving slices from stalk to the base, turning the pepper as you go, remove the flesh. The seeds will remain attached to the stalk. Some useful pieces may remain around the stalk. Cut with the inside upwards as the shiny outside is rather tough.

Red, yellow and orange peppers are tastier than the green.

BREADED PORK ESCALOPES WITH HAM AND CHEESE

Emmental or Gruyere cheese are the ideal for this recipe but it is almost as good with mature cheddar. This is quite a fiddly recipe so if you're entertaining I would do most of the preparation beforehand

To do beforehand:-
Up to stage 5 in the recipe and refrigerate until needed. Remove from the fridge 1 hour before cooking.

750g pork fillet
4 slices of ham
250g Emmental, gruyere or cheddar cheese cut into thin slices
Seasoned flour - 300g flour with 1 level teaspoon of salt and a good grinding of black pepper
1 egg whisked together with 2 tablespoons of milk
white breadcrumbs

1. Cutting across the pork fillet cut into 4cm thick pieces and then cutting the same way almost cut each piece in half by cutting almost through but leaving a hinge.
2. With each piece of meat open out the flaps and place flat on a piece of cling film. Cover with cling film and with a wine bottle or rolling pin bash the meat until it is rather thin - about ½ cm thick.
3. Cover one half of the meat with a slice of ham and on top of this a covering of cheese - not quite to the edge.
4. Pull the other half of the meat over to cover the filling - just like a sandwich. Press well together.
5. Place each piece in the flour and coat on both sides, then dip in the egg and then the crumbs - press them on well.
6. Put 1 tablespoon of olive oil with 1 knob of butter in a frying pan to heat up. When hot add the escalopes, or however many you can fit in the pan, and fry on medium heat for 2-3 minutes. When browned, turn over and cook the same on the other side. Keep them

warm in a low oven whilst frying the next lot.

SALMON EN CROUTE - Salmon in a puff pastry parcel

An ideal dish when entertaining as it can be all wrapped up ready, placed in the fridge and ready to cook when required.
Also it wouldn't be a sin to omit potatoes from your menu with this as there is quite a lot of pastry. Serve with a couple of nice vegetables or one vegetable and a salad.

To do beforehand:-
All of this recipe can be prepared and kept in the fridge until 1 hour before you need to bake it.

Preheat oven 200C fan 220C electric and 7 gas

1 piece of salmon fillet per person (about 175g)
1 packet of Saxby's all butter puff pastry (375g)
1 egg - beaten
4 spring onions
small tub of crème fraîche (300)g
2 teasp. of horseradish sauce
grated rind of 1 lemon
1 teasp. lemon juice
1 teasp. of runny honey
1 tabsp. tomato ketchup

1. Firstly skin the salmon with the skin side on the board by gripping one end of the skin and running a very sharp knife between the skin and the flesh from the end you are holding, keeping the knife slanting towards the skin.
2. Finely chop the spring onions and place in a bowl with a good knob of butter (30g) and microwave on high for 2 minutes.
3. Mix all of the last ingredients from the crème fraîche to the ketchup and add a pinch of salt and a grinding of

black pepper. Taste - if too sharp add a little more honey.
4. Cut the puff pastry into 4 squares and roll out on a floured surface until they are oblong in shape and approximately 13x18cm
5. Beat the egg well and paint round the outer edge of the pastry with your finger.
6. Dollop a full teaspoon of the crème fraîche mix on ½ of the pastry where the fish will go and put the fish on top.
7. Put an equal amount of spring onions over the top of each piece of fish and also 2 teaspoonfuls of the crème fraîche mixture.
8. Pull the other side of the pastry over the salmon and seal down to the other side, also sealing the ends. Press down well.
9. With a brush or finger paint all over the top with the beaten egg and make a couple of small holes in the top of each.
10. Place on a greased baking tray and place in the fridge until required. Remove one hour before cooking.
11. Place in the oven for 20 - 25 minutes. Keep an eye that they don't brown too quickly so that you can reduce the heat if needed.

SPARE-RIB PORK CHOPS IN CIDER AND CREAM SAUCE

To do beforehand:-
This dish can be completely prepared and chilled for up to a couple of days, removing from the fridge an hour before it is to be heated. It will need about 30-40 minutes at the temperature below to heat through.

1 medium onion peeled and finely chopped
olive oil for browning the chops
4 spare-rib pork chops
salt and pepper
1 litre strong cider

vegetable stock powder or 1 cube to mix into the cider
1 rounded tabsp. cornflour
2 tabsp. cold water
small carton double cream (150ml)
4 red eating apples for decoration

Preheat oven   180C fan 200C electric or 6 gas

1. Choose a casserole or deep baking tin which will just hold the pork chops in one layer.
2. Sprinkle the chopped onion over the bottom.
3. Salt and pepper the chops on both sides and in some hot oil in a frying pan, brown them quickly on high heat on both sides and arrange on top of the onion.
4. Heat the cider a little in the microwave not forgetting to add the vegetable stock cube or powder, and pour over the chops - it should almost cover them.
5. Cover with foil or a lid and place in the oven.
6. After 20 minutes turn the oven down to 120C fan 140C electric or 1 gas
7. Whilst the pork is cooking prepare the apple garnish. Wash and ¼ them and remove the core. Cut into slices and arrange neatly overlapping in 4 groups on a plate. Cover with clingfilm, pierce in two places and then put in the microwave for 1 to 2 minutes to cook.
8. Cook the pork for 2½ hours and then remove from the oven.
9. Drain the liquid off into a saucepan and heat on the stove. When boiling, add a little of the cornflour which has been mixed with the water. Don't add it all at once as you may not need it all to thicken it. When it reboils it should be about as thick as custard. Allow to boil on low heat to cook the cornflour.
10. Take the sauce off the heat and stir in the cream. Taste to check for enough salt and pepper.
11. Pour the sauce back over the pork chops and lay the apple pieces neatly on the top of each chop.
12. Cover and return to the oven to heat through.

CHICKEN SALTIMBOCCA

Simple but very tasty - chicken wrapped in dry cured ham.

To do beforehand:-
Prepare up to and including stage 4 in the recipe, place on a plate and chill.
(cocktail sticks for fixing)
4 boneless chicken breasts
8 slices Black Forest ham (Aldi or Lidle)
8 sage leaves (optional)
freshly ground black pepper
Flour
30gm butter
1 tabsp. olive oil
150ml white wine
Small carton (150ml) double cream

1. Halve the chicken breasts crossways with a slanting cut.
2. Place each piece of meat between two pieces of cling film and with a rolling pin or wine bottle pound flat till 1cm thick.
3. Wrap each piece with a slice of ham with the join underneath and a sage leaf on the top.
4. With a cocktail stick and one in and out move, fix the leaf down and fix the ham together underneath.
5. Prepare some seasoned flour on a plate by mixing a good grinding of black pepper with two tablespoons of flour. The ham should make the chicken salty enough.
6. Lightly coat with the flour both sides of each piece of chicken, shaking off any excess.
7. Heat half of the oil and butter in a frying pan and fry the chicken for about 2 minutes on each side and keep warm whilst you repeat by adding the remaining oil and butter to the pan to cook the remaining chicken. Lift out and keep warm.
8. Pour the white wine into the pan and allow to boil for a

few minutes until there is only a little liquid left.
9. On low heat, add the cream to this and with a suitable utensil, scrape all the sediment off the bottom of the pan into the sauce - this will give good flavour.
10. Serve two pieces of meat per person on warmed plates and pour the sauce over.

BRAISED LAMB SHANKS IN RED WINE

To do beforehand:-
This can all be cooked beforehand and reheated when required. If doing this, after the first cooking gently lift the shanks out of the liquid and keep separate. Keep refrigerated. Allow to come up to room temperature for about 2 hours before reheating. To reheat, bring the liquid to a boil in a flameproof casserole and then gently lower in the lamb. Cover with a lid or foil and place in the oven which has been preheated to 180C fan 200 electric or 6 gas and heat for 40-45 minutes.

Preheat oven - 200C fan 220 electric or 7 gas

Olive oil
4 lamb shanks
2 medium onions - sliced
2 medium carrots, peeled and sliced - 1cm thick
4 cloves of garlic - peeled and thinly sliced
500ml vegetable stock
500ml red wine
2 tabsp. balsamic vinegar
2 rounded teasp. sugar (brown if you have it)
2 bay leaves
2 sprigs of fresh rosemary (or a sprinkling of dried mixed herbs)
good grinding of black pepper
level teasp. salt

1. Choose a lidded, metal casserole if you have one, if not

a deep strong roasting tin will do topped off with foil.
2. Dribble some olive oil over the shanks and with both hands work it all over the meat.
3. Place the 4 shanks in the casserole and when the oven has come up to heat, put them in without a lid to sizzle for 30 minutes.
4. After this time they should have browned nicely. Remove from the oven and lift out of the casserole.
5. Turn the oven down to 130C fan 150 electric or gas 2.
6. Place the casserole on the stove on high heat and add the onions and carrots, allowing them to brown.
7. Add the garlic and the two rounded tablespoons of flour. Stir on low heat for 1 minute.
8. Add a little of the vegetable stock and mix in well allowing to heat through and boil. Add the remaining stock and allow to reboil. Taste for pepper and salt.
9. Add all of the remaining ingredients, mix well and drop the lamb shanks gently into the liquid.
10. Bring back to a boil, put the lid on or top with the foil, sealing round the edges and place in the oven.
11. After 20 minutes turn the oven down to 120C fan 140C electric or 1 gas. Cook for 3 hours.

Hints

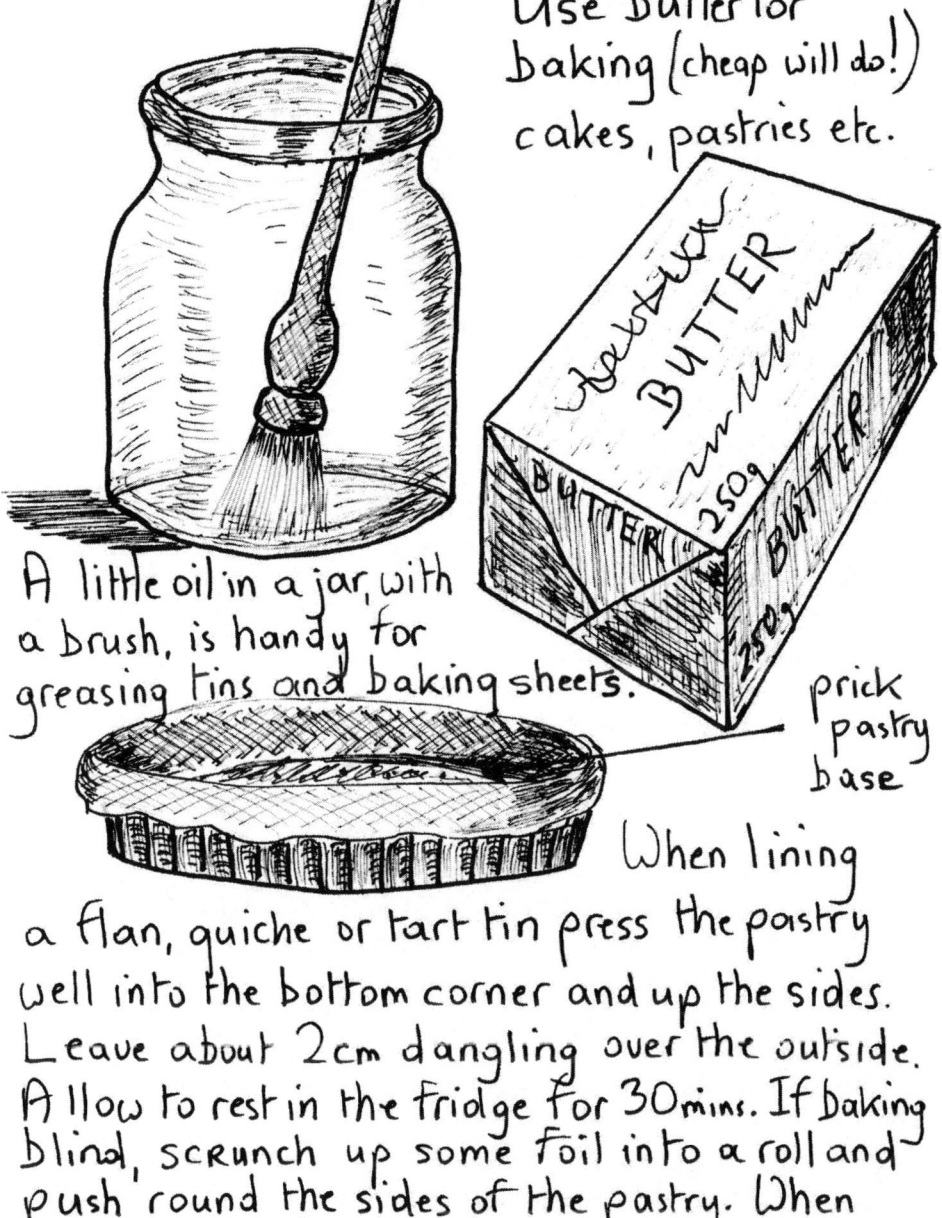

Use butter for baking (cheap will do!) cakes, pastries etc.

A little oil in a jar, with a brush, is handy for greasing tins and baking sheets.

prick pastry base

When lining a flan, quiche or tart tin press the pastry well into the bottom corner and up the sides. Leave about 2cm dangling over the outside. Allow to rest in the fridge for 30mins. If baking blind, scrunch up some foil into a roll and push 'round the sides of the pastry. When finally cooked trim the pastry to the tin's edge

Sweets, Puddings etc.

BANOFFI PIE (courtesy of Carnation condensed milk)

This recipe is an improvement on my original for which I could most likely have been charged with *inciting an act of explosion*. The original recipes for this involved placing the unopened tins (I would do three at a time to have some in reserve) in a saucepan and covering them with water. The tins were then boiled gently for 2 hours and it was important to keep checking that the water was covering the tins! I must admit that I never felt that this was a safe process!
Banoffi pie can also be made with a ready-made or home-made pastry tart base.

275g butter (100g for the base)
250g gingernut biscuits (digestive biscuits work well also)
175g caster sugar
397g tin condensed milk
2 bananas
150ml whipped double cream
Grated plain chocolate

1. In the microwave gently melt 100g of the butter and stir in the crushed biscuits. Press into the base and sides of a 19cm. loose bottomed flan tin.
2. Place the remaining butter and sugar in a non stick saucepan over a low heat, stirring until the butter melts. Add the condensed milk and bring gently to the boil, stirring continuously. Boil steadily for 5 minutes stirring frequently, to make a light golden caramel.
3. Pour over the biscuit base and chill for about 1½ hours, until firm
4. Slice the bananas and arrange over the top. Cover with the whipped cream and sprinkle over the grated chocolate.

SHORTBREAD FRIUT TART

Shortbread, as recipe page 145, rolled out into one large round, made up into one round that has already been cut into sections or individual shortbread biscuits as a base.

250gm tub of mascarpone
2 tabsp. of crème fraîche
½ teasp. vanilla essence
Soft fruit of your choice - blackberries, raspberries, strawberries, blueberries etc.
Icing sugar

1. Beat together the mascarpone, crème fraîche and vanilla essence.
2. Pipe or spread it onto the shortbread.
3. Arrange the fruit on top.
4. With the aid of a fine sieve, dust some icing sugar over the top - the amount will depend on how much sweetening you think the fruit needs.

ORANGE CHEESE CAKE

For 12 or 6 persons.
This is rather large for normal family food. For everyday I would use a 17cm - 20cm tin and halve the quantities and use a small tin of evaporated milk.

Preheat oven 160C fan 180C electric or 4 gas
Loose bottomed 23cm cake or deep flan tin

Base - 225gm digestive biscuits
85gm butter

Filling - 1 large tin (410gm) evaporated milk (chilled for 24 hours)
1 packet orange jelly

100ml boiling water
2 large packets (300g) of soft cheese
1 tablespoon caster sugar

For decorating - optional
Double cream - whipped or for pouring.
Plain chocolate - grated

1. Crush the biscuits.
2. Melt the butter in a bowl in the microwave
3. Mix the biscuits into the butter and tip into the base of the tin. Spread out evenly and press down.
4. Bake in the oven for 10 minutes and allow to cool.
5. Dissolve the jelly in the hot water, if not completely dissolved, finish in the microwave. Put to one side to cool.
6. Whisk the evaporated milk till very thick.
7. Beat together the soft cheese and sugar.
8. Add 2 large spoonfuls of the milk to the cheese and gently mix in.
9. When the jelly is cool but not quite set mix it with the remaining evaporated milk into the cheese mixture.
10. Pour into the tin on top of the biscuit base and chill for 24 hours.
11. Remove gently from the tin and decorate with some whipped cream and grated plain chocolate if liked or simply served with cream.

REALLY EASY VANILLA ICE

1 large tin (410gm) evaporated milk (chilled in the fridge for 24 hours at least)
1 300gm carton double cream (best) OR 300ml cold thick custard OR a tin of good quality custard
3 rounded tabsp. caster sugar
½ teasp. vanilla essence

1. Whisk up the evaporated milk as thick as it will go.
2. Whisk the double cream and the vanilla essence till ¾ thick but not as thick as for piping!
3. Sprinkle the sugar over the top of the evaporated milk.
4. With a large metal spoon gently fold 2 spoonfuls of the milk into the cream trying not to knock too much of the air out!
5. Finally tip the cream mix into the milk and gently mix it all together by folding which is best explained by not mixing but gently turning the mixture over, turning the bowl a little at a time inbetween each move!
6. Scrape the mix out gently into a suitable lidded container and place in the freezer for 24 hours.

SAUCE for ICECREAM:-

Chocolate -

125g dark chocolate
1 (170g) tin of evaporated milk
1 rounded tablespoon caster sugar

Place the broken chocolate, evaporated milk and sugar altogether in a bowl and microwave for 1 minute on high. Remove and stir well. If the chocolate needs more melting, return and heat in 30 second bursts until all have dissolved together. Serve hot.

Caramel -

150g soft brown sugar
100g butter
2 tabsp. golden syrup (standing the spoon in boiling water beforehand will help with measuring out the syrup)
Small carton double cream (150ml)

Place all except the cream in a bowl and microwave on

high for 1 minute. Mix well and continue heating in short bursts until all has dissolved and mixed well. Add the cream, mix well and heat a little more if liked.

FRESH FRUIT RIPPLE

225gm (8oz) of fruit – raspberries and strawberries are best but other suitable fruits could be apricots, peaches, blackcurrants, gooseberries etc. Fruit such as blackberries and gooseberries will need cooking with some sweetening first.
1 rounded tablespoon sugar – can vary with different fruits and according to your taste
1 tin(425g) good quality custard OR some cold *thickish* homemade custard (500ml).
1 carton(300ml) double OR whipping cream

1. If using raspberries or strawberries gently wash the fruit by either placing it in a large sieve or a colander and holding the fruit under cold running water. Preparation of other fruit will be different and so I have explained this at the end of the recipe.
2. If using strawberries, remove the hulls (green bits) and slice up roughly.
3. Place the fruit and sugar in a liquidiser or food processor (with the blade) and allow to pulp down – not leaving the machine on too long as it will become too liquid – it's better with a few small lumps of fruit in it. If your family balk at the raspberry seeds you will need to put the sauce through a sieve at this stage.
4. Whip the cream until ¾ stiff and then gently mix in the custard.
5. Put the fruit sauce in a jug and if you don't have a piping bag, place the cream mixture in a small, clean polythene bag and with scissors cut one of the bottom corners off to make a 1cm(1/2 inch) hole, winding the top end round to keep the *goo* in!

6. Use 4 small straight sided glasses. Squeeze a layer of the cream mixture to cover the base and then pour in a thin layer of fruit sauce. Repeat this, finishing with a *twirl* of the cream mixture.

OTHER FRUITS
Peaches and apricots – these need 'blanching' so that the skin can be removed. Place in a bowl or saucepan and cover with boiling water for 1 minute. Drain off the water and the skins should pull off easily with the aid of a small pointed knife. Remove the stones by cutting down the 'crease' in the fruit and round the other side. If the fruit is ripe the stoned should be easy to remove by twisting each half of the fruit in opposite directions. If the fruit is ripe you can chop it roughly and carry on from stage 3. If you feel that it is a little hard – *cook it a little first with a tablespoon of water and the sugar, in a lidded pan on low heat. When cool it can then be liquidised, adding more sugar if needed.
Blackcurrant and Gooseberries Wash the fruit and then *top and tail* – cut off the stalk and *bit* at the bottom of the fruit, and then carry on from * as above.

CHOCOLATE MOUSSE

This recipe uses marshmallows, to help get some air into the mixture instead of raw eggs which can be a bit of a *no no* these days.

60g butter
250g plain chocolate (not cooking chocolate)
140ml boiling milk
150g marshmallows (small if possible, if not, take a sharp knife which has been dipped in boiling water and ¼ some large ones.
300ml double OR whipping cream
½ teasp. vanilla essence

1. Put the butter, broken up chocolate and milk in a

largish bowl.
2. If the hot milk doesn't melt the chocolate and butter so that it can be well mixed, give it a short burst in the microwave. Only 30 seconds at a time and stirring in-between until all has melted.
3. Gently mix in the marshmallows until they have melted into the mix. Use the microwave to warm the mix a little if the marshmallows don't dissolve.
4. Whip the cream with 2 drops of vanilla essence to ¾ stiff not piping stiff.
5. Tip the chocolate mix onto the cream and gently fold in.
6. Pour into individual dishes or glasses.

TRADITIONAL SHERRY TRIFLE

It is so easy to make your own sponge rather than buying it and of course it tastes a lot nicer. It can quickly be made in the microwave.

1 packet of trifle sponges OR some homemade sponge - microwaved syrup sponge without the syrup.
raspberry or strawberry jam
1 tin of raspberries
150ml sherry
300ml thick custard or 1 large tin of good quality custard
300ml double or whipping cream
grated chocolate (optional) for decoration

1. If you are making your own custard do this first because it needs to be cold. Cover it with clingfilm to stop a skin forming.
2. If making your own sponge, do this, and tip out onto a wire rack to cool.
3. When the sponge is cold, slice it into 4 *crossways* so that you have 4 disks - take the 2 smallest and then the 2 largest and sandwich them together with the jam. Packet sponges need to be split in half and spread with jam.

4. In a suitable glass dish, arrange the sponge which has been cut into 1.5cm slices. You might have two layers of sponge - this will be OK.
5. Put the sherry with half of the fruit juice in a small jug and pour it evenly over the sponge.
6. If the sponge isn't really moist, use more of the juice
7. Whip the cream up - ¾ *thick* and reserve a little for decorating the top.
8. Mix the larger amount of cream with the custard and pour it evenly over the top of the sponge.
9. Decorate the top with the remaining cream, which will need whipping a little more, and the grated chocolate.

CARAMELISED UPSIDE DOWN FRUIT TART (Tarte Tatin)

This is a delicious and simple recipe to do. Serve with vanilla ice, crème fraîche or cream. Dessert apples, pears and plums are some of the fruits suitable for this recipe.

Preheat oven   200C fan   220C electric or 7 gas

85g butter
170g soft brown sugar
4 - 5 good sized dessert apples
grated zest and juice of one lemon
1 packet Saxby's all butter puff pastry

1. In a 26cm (approximately) non stick frying pan which has an ovenproof handle, put the butter and sugar on low heat and stir till the sugar has dissolved.
2. Leave on low heat for another 3 minutes.
3. Grate the lemon rind finely (not as far down as the white pith) and juice the lemon. Put both in a basin large enough to take the prepared apples.
4. Peel, core and slice the apples into neat sections (about 8 per apple) and toss them in the lemon juice and zest - this will stop them going brown.
5. Arrange the apple pieces neatly in the sugar and butter

mixture around the base of the pan - covering it totally.
6. Roll out the pastry on a floured surface, if possible into a round shape the size of the frying pan. This is possible if between each roll you turn the pastry round clockwise a little. If you repeat this each time the pastry will be round rather than square.
7. The easy way to transfer the pastry to on top of the apples is to flour it lightly and then gently wrap it round the rolling pin. Gently unroll it over the top of the apples.
8. Tuck the pastry down the insides of the pan and over the apples. Trim off any excess
9. Place in the oven and turn down the heat after 10 minutes to 160fan 180electric or 4 gas.
10. It should take about 25 - 30 minutes to cook and should be golden brown.
11. Remove from the oven and leave to stand for 10 minutes.
12. Place a warm serving dish upside down over the pan and turn all over to tip out the tart with the fruit uppermost.

LEMON DELIGHT

The *delight* in this recipe is the delicious lemony sauce that forms underneath the sponge topping.

Preheat oven   170C fan 190C electric or 5 gas
Medium sized greased ovenproof dish

170g caster sugar
60g butter
1 lemon - grated rind and juice
60g self raising flour
1 rounded teasp. baking powder
2 eggs - separated - yolk from white
275ml milk

1. In a bowl beat the sugar and butter together until pale and creamy.
2. Add the grated rind and juice of one lemon.
3. Sieve together the flour and baking powder and add.
4. Lightly beat the egg yolks with the milk and mix in till all is well mixed.
5. Beat the eggs whites until ¾ stiff (if done too stiffly they will be difficult to mix in).
6. Fold in gently the beaten egg whites and pour into a well greased dish.
7. Stand this in a larger dish which has been filled to half way up with hot water.
8. Bake for 30 - 40 minutes - when the top is gently pressed with a finger it should feel set.

APPLE BATTER

110g plain flour
1 egg
275ml milk
Small pinch of salt
1 tabsp. sunflower oil
2 cooking apples or 4 eaters
sugar or warm syrup for serving.

Preheat oven 200C fan 220C electric or 7 gas

1. Firstly make the batter by sieving the flour into a bowl with the salt.
2. Make a hole in the centre and beat half of the milk with the egg and pour into this hole
3. With a fork or a whisk slowly bring in the flour from round the edge mixing it in well.
4. When the mixture is becoming thick adding a little of the remaining milk at a time, gradually mixing in the remaining flour.
5. Put the oil in a metal baking dish (small roasting tin) and place in the oven to heat up.

6. Peel and core the apples and cut into chunks about 1½cm thick and keep in water which has a squeeze of lemon juice in to stop the apples browning.
7. After 15 - 20 minutes in the oven the dish should be hot enough but before getting it out of the oven, drain the apple pieces and dry on kitchen paper.
8. Gently drop the apple into the hot tin, and then give the batter a mix up before pouring in with the apples. If possible spread the apples around evenly and return to the oven.
9. Bake for 20 minutes before lowering the heat to 140C fan   160C electric or 3 gas.
10. It will probably take a further 10 - 15 minutes.
11. Serve either sprinkled with granulated sugar or warmed syrup or honey.

BREAD AND BUTTER PUDDING

30g sultanas
2 slices of white bread - well buttered
3 large eggs
50g caster sugar
½ teasp. vanilla essence
500ml milk

Preheat oven   140C fan   160C electric or 3 gas

1. Grease a medium sized pie dish and sprinkle the sultanas over the bottom
2. If wished you can remove the crusts from the bread and then cut each slice into 4 triangles and arrange neatly overlapping in the dish.
3. Take the chill off the milk by warming it for 1 minute in the microwave.
4. Whisk the eggs, sugar and essence together and pour the warmed milk on, mixing well.
5. Sprinkle with granulated sugar.
6. If liked, sprinkle the top with ground or freshly grated

nutmeg.
7. Stand in a roasting tin half full of hot water and cook in the oven for about 45 minutes - until the pudding has set.

BASIC BAKED CHEESECAKE

Preheat oven 160 fan 180 electric or 4 gas

20cm round loose bottomed tin

This is a cheesecake with only vanilla essence to flavour it but it can of course be adapted to other flavours with the appropriate additions - orange or lemon juice, chocolate, sultanas, blueberries etc. Believe me, it is delicious simply left plain.

30gm butter (melted)
150gm digestive biscuits, crushed
2 large packets (250gm) of cream cheese
150gm caster sugar
1 teasp. vanilla essence
2 large eggs, beaten
1 small carton (150ml) double cream
1 rounded tablespoon (35gm) cornflour

1. Brush the melted butter liberally around the tin and place in the fridge for 15 minutes. Repeat this once more to make a thicker layer of butter.
2. When the butter has set a little on the tin, sprinkle a shallow layer (½ cm) of biscuit over the base and press down.
3. With the fingers press some of the crumbs up the side of the tin.
4. Place the cheese, sugar and vanilla in bowl and beat well, this can be done in a processor or mixer.
5. With a fork mix the cornflour into one third of the cream

6. Beat together the remaining cream and eggs. Add to this the cornfour mix and stir well.
7. Finally add the egg mix to the cheese one and blend together thoroughly.
8. Pour the mix into the tin and sprinkle the remaining biscuit crumbs over the top
9. Bake for 40 minutes, don't open the oven but switch off the heat and leave for another 45 minutes to allow the cake to set off.
10. Remove from the oven and cool in the tin.

Serve with a good dollop of crème fraîche or single cream.

BAKEWELL TART - a family favourite

Ground almonds are expensive but do improve the texture of the filling. Unfortunately they don't usually taste very *almondy* and so it is always necessary to add a few drops of almond essence. If you are on a tight budget substitute the almonds with semolina or ground rice.

Preheat oven   180C fan 200C electric or 6 gas

20cm tart or flan tin

Sweet pastry as in the Pastry, Cakes and Biscuits section.

Almond filling:-
110g butter
110g caster sugar
2 beaten eggs
60g ground almonds (or substitute with semolina or ground rice)
60g flour
almond essence
raspberry, strawberry or apricot jam

Desserts and Pastry

A few desserts, such as trifle, are best served in a glass bowl.

Many desserts such as fruit fool, mousse, jelly etc. look good in a glass.

Tarts and quiches are best baked in a tin to achieve CRISPNESS.

For cheesecakes, bake the biscuit and butter base on medium heat for 10-15 minutes.
This helps to prevent the topping from turning the base soggy.

1. Line a greased 20cm round tin with the pastry (page 137) or buy a ready made pastry case. If you are lining a tin with your own pastry, flatten it in your hands, wrap it in clingfilm and place in the fridge for 15 - 20 minutes. Roll the pastry out into a rough circle which is 2cm bigger all round the tin. Roll it gently round the rolling pin and then roll it out over the tin. Working round the tin, gently ease the pastry down the side of the tin, pressing it into the bottom corner and to the side of the tin. Allow the spare to hang over the top and down the outside - this will be trimmed off later.
2. Place in the fridge again until you have the filling ready. This will help the pastry to keep it's shape when cooked.
3. If you have made your own pastry pierce the base with a fork in a few places.
4. Spread the raspberry jam over the bottom, fairly liberally.
5. Make the filling by beating together (hand or machine) the softened butter and sugar till pale and creamy coloured.
6. Add 2 or 3 drops of almond essence to the eggs.
7. Beat in the eggs a little at a time adding a little of the flour and almonds (or substitute) at the same time - beat well between each addition.
8. If you cannot smell the almond flavour, beat in a little more at this stage.
9. Finally gently mix in the remaining flour and almonds.
10. Spread evenly over the jam in the pastry case.
11. Bake for about 30 minutes until, when gently pressed with a finger, the filling springs back.
12. After the tart has cooled for 10 minutes, trim the pastry round the edge of the tin with a sharp knife.
13. Best served with custard.

APPLE PIE

A tin pie plate (20cm) is best for this so that the underneath pastry cooks. Glass or pottery don't get hot enough. This recipe can be adapted to any fruit - prepared fresh fruit or well drained tinned. Some recipes suggest cooking the fruit first but this will only make the base soggy.

1 quantity of shortcrust pastry (page 136) Before rolling it out allow to *rest,* wrapped in clingfilm, in the fridge for about 20 minutes.
2 large cooking apples, peeled, cored and sliced.
2 tabsp. sugar (brown if you have it)
a little grated lemon rind
juice from ½ lemon
Additions - add any of these if you fancy them - a sprinkling of ground cinnamon or nutmeg or a handful of sultanas.

Preheat oven 180C fan 200 electric or 6 gas

1. In a bowl place the rind and juice of the lemon - this is ready for the apples as you prepare them so that you can stir them around as you add more so that the covering of lemon juice will stop them from browning.
2. Divide the pastry in half with just a little more for the top than the bottom.
3. Grease the tin and roll out the pastry to fit with a little to spare.
4. Before putting the fruit on, roll out the top so that it is ready - making sure that it is a little larger than the bottom.
5. Drain the apple and mix with the sugar.
6. Place on the pastry and with a finger wet around the edge with water.
7. Place the top on - rolling it around the pin is the easiest way to lift it.
8. Press well all around the edge and crimp with a fork or

your fingers.
9. Brush with a little milk and sprinkle liberally with granulated sugar.
10. Make a small hole in the centre and place in the oven.
11. After 15 minutes reduce the heat to 140C fan 160C electric or 3 gas.
12. To ensure that the fruit is cooked it will probably take another 25 minutes.

BAKED FRUIT SPONGE

A basic sponge mixture topping for a fruit of your choice - either fresh or tinned.

1 tin sliced peaches, apricot halves, pineapple etc.
OR prepared fruit - apples, pears, plums etc.
115g caster sugar
115g butter (at room temperature)
2 large eggs lightly beaten
½ teasp. vanilla essence
115g self raising flour
1 rounded teasp. baking powder

Preheat oven 160C fan 180 electric or 5 gas

The fresh fruit simply needs peeling, coring or stoning and can be cooked from raw. Large fruit can be sliced and all should be mixed with some sugar.

1. Grease a suitable dish and lay the fruit over the base.
2. Beat the butter and sugar together using an electric beater or a wooden spoon.
3. Add the vanilla essence and mix in well.
4. Sieve the flour and the baking powder together.
5. Add a little egg at a time with a sprinkling of flour, beating well between each addition.
6. Finally gently fold in the remaining flour with a metal spoon.
7. Spoon the sponge on top of the fruit in small blobs

which when cooked will merge into one another
8. Bake for about 30 minutes, making sure that the fruit is cooked.

SYRUP SPONGE PUDDING

Traditionally this would be steamed but nowadays the ideal way to cook it is in the microwave.

150g self raising flour
1 rounded teasp. baking powder
85g soft butter
85g sugar
1 egg
3 tabsp. milk
½ teasp. vanilla essence
2 good tabsp. golden syrup

1. Grease a suitable pudding basin and put the syrup in the bottom. Stand the spoon in boiling water to heat up before wiping it dry and then measuring out the syrup. It slips off the spoon easier this way.
2. Sieve the flour and baking powder into a bowl and add the remaining ingredients. Beat together well. This can be done in a food processor.
3. Turn the mixture into the basin on top of the syrup and level off. The mixture shouldn't come more than ¾ up the basin.
4. Cover loosely with greaseproof or kitchen paper.
5. Cook in the microwave on high for 4 minutes. This timing will vary because the power varies from microwave to microwave.
6. If it doesn't look cooked do not move it but cook on high for a further 1- 2 minutes. The first one you make will be a bit experimental - make a note on the recipe about the cooking time.
7. Allow to stand for 2 minutes before running a knife round the edge and then tipping out carefully.

Pastry, Cakes and Biscuits

PASTRY

I'm sure that by the time I get around to finishing this book there will be some very good all butter pastry available to buy whereas at the moment a lot of them contain chemically engineered fats which are harmful to health.

PUFF PASTRY

The simple option is to buy this as it is difficult to make successfully. When I was at catering college, students practised the making of this for a week, and in some cases at the end of the week, some hadn't mastered the art of getting it to rise! I prefer Saxby's all butter puff pastry.

FILO PASTRY

This pastry is very versatile and can be used for a variety of sweet and savoury dishes. My advice is to buy it!

SHORT PASTRY

200g plain flour
100g cold butter
2-3 tabsp. cold water

1. Weigh the flour and then coarse grate the butter on top of it.
2. Tip into a bowl and with the tips of the fingers gently rub the fat into the flour - don't handle more than necessary. The mix should look sandy.
3. Add half the cold water and mix with a fork, pressing the ingredients together gently.
4. Add more water until all the mix comes together.
5. Finish with the fingers, wrap in cling film and allow to

rest in the fridge for 20 minutes before using.

FLAN PASTRY - for savoury flans and quiches

200g plain flour
100g cold butter
1 beaten egg

1. Start as if making short pastry in stages 1 and 2.
2. Add the beaten egg and mix in as with the short pastry.
3. As you're adding the egg - if you feel that the mix is a little dry, add a little cold water. The mix mustn't be wet.
4. As with short pastry, wrap in clingfilm and allow a 20 minute rest in the fridge before use.

SWEET PASTRY - for sweet tarts and flans

125g butter (at room temperature)
50g sugar
200g plain flour
1   beaten egg

1. In a bowl with a wooden spoon mix the butter and sugar together until creamy.
2. Add a small spoon of flour and half the egg - mix well
3. Repeat with another small spoon of flour and the remaining egg.
4. Add the remaining flour and mix in well.
5. Everything should come together - wrap in cling film - rest for 20 minutes in the fridge before using.

TRADITIONAL SPONGE CAKE

Preheat the oven to 180 fan 200 electric or 6 gas

Lightly grease 2 x 20cm cake tins and put a circle of non-stick baking parchment in the base of each

CHOCOLATE SPONGE - to adapt this recipe to make a chocolate sponge - replace 30 grams of flour with 30 grams of cocoa powder and cut out the vanilla essence.

170g butter (at room temperature)
170g caster sugar
3 large eggs lightly beaten
170g self raising flour
2 rounded teaspoons baking powder
½ teaspoon vanilla essence

1. Beat the butter and sugar together using an electric beater or a wooden spoon.
2. Add the vanilla essence.
3. Sieve the flour and baking powder together.
4. Add a little egg at a time with a sprinkling of flour, beating well between each addition.
5. Finally gently fold in the rest of the flour with a large metal spoon.
6. Divide the mix between the two tins and level gently
7. Place in the oven (centre if not fan) and bake for about 20 - 25 minutes. When gently pressing the top the cake should spring back when it is cooked.
8. Leave in the tins for 2 to 3 minutes and then tip out onto a cooling rack and gently peel off the paper.
9. Sandwich together with jam or butter cream or both.

BUTTER CREAM

In a bowl place 90 grams of softened butter (unsalted or lightly salted) and with a wooden spoon or with an electric beater, mix vigorously. Add a couple of drops of vanilla essence. Sift 90 grams of icing sugar and adding a little at a time, beat well in between. Beat until light and creamy. To make the mix less rich, beat in gradually one table spoon of cold boiled water.

FAIRY or CUP CAKES

This is an easy recipe as all the ingredients can be mixed together in a food processor or mixer with a beater attachment. The alternative is to place all the ingredients together in a large bowl and mixing well with a wooden spoon.

Preheat the oven to 160C fan 180C electric or 4 gas. Place 12 cake cases in a 12 cup bun tin.

All ingredients should be at room temperature
110g self-raising flour
1 rounded teasp. baking powder
110g caster sugar
110g softened butter
2 eggs lightly beaten
1 tabsp. milk

1. Sift together the flour and baking powder.
2. Place all the ingredients together except the milk and mix well in a processor, mixer or by hand with a wooden spoon.
3. Add the milk and mix again.
4. Divide the mix equally between the cake cases.
5. Bake for 15-20 minutes until risen and firm to the touch., turning after 15 minutes so that they cook evenly - do this gently, leaving the oven door open for as short a time as is possible.
6. Allow to cool a little and then place on a wire rack.
7. Decorate as wished when cold. Ordinary icing is the most common topping and this can be done in many colours and flavours and decorated with 'sprinkles' of varying sorts.

CHOCOLATE FRIDGE CAKE

So easy that I was fortunate to get this in lieu of a Birthday Cake from my ageing Mum when she had almost given up on everyday cooking! It is very sweet but very *moreish* and should be cut into thin slices.

A 150cm cake tin greased and lined with one piece of cling film covering the base and the sides.

340g good plain chocolate broken into pieces (½ for in the cake and ½ to coat the outside)
115 butter
1 (397g) tin of condensed milk
280g crushed rich tea biscuits (not as fine as dust!)
30g sultanas or raisins
6 half walnuts for decoration

1. This can either be done in the microwave or on a low heat on the top of the stove. Melt half the chocolate with the condensed milk and the butter. Don't overheat and mix well.
2. Stir in the biscuits and the raisins and stir in well.
3. Tip into the cake tin (lined with clingfilm) pushing the mix down and levelling off the top.
4. Chill in the fridge for at least 8 hours.
5. When removed from the tin and cling film removed, melt the remaining chocolate, breaking it in pieces and in a suitable bowl, with short bursts, in the microwave and only heating in short blasts. Pour the chocolate onto the centre of the cake and with a large knife or palette knife spread the chocolate all over the cake - also down the sides.
6. If liked decorate the top with 6 walnut halves.
7. Keep cool. Best eaten in small slices!

Cakes

Tray bakes are ideal for family cooking. A tin of approximately 20cm x 30cm will make a good quantity

To make half the amount use a tin measuring about 17cm x 17cm

CARROT CAKE

Preheat the oven to 160 fan 180 electric or 4 gas

18cm square tin - lined with baking parchment - if just covering the base, grease the sides well.

3 eggs lightly beaten
175ml of sunflower oil
175g soft light brown sugar
175g self-raising flour
2 rounded teaspoons baking powder
1 level teaspoon ground cinnamon
1 level teaspoon ground nutmeg
3 medium peeled and coarsely grated carrots
100g raisins or sultanas
Grated zest of 1 orange (wash and dry the orange thoroughly before grating the zest only just to the white pith with a microplane or fine grater).

1. Place the eggs, sugar and oil in a bowl and mix well with a whisk.
2. Sieve altogether the flour, baking powder, cinnamon and nutmeg
3. Add the flour mix to the bowl and mix well
4. Then add the last 3 ingredients - orange zest, grated carrots and raisins and stir in.
5. Pour the mix into the prepared tin and bake for about 40 - 50 minutes until the top feels firm to the touch.
6. Allow to cool for a few minutes and then turn out onto a wire rack. Peel off the paper.
7. When cold spread with the topping.

CARROT CAKE TOPPING

50gm butter (at room temperature)
150gm cream cheese
50gm sifted icing sugar
½ teaspoon vanilla essence

Beat the butter and the cream cheese together and then add the essence and icing sugar. Beat till light and creamy.

MOIST GINGER CAKE (GINGERBREAD)

If possible cook a few days before required as this cake improves with keeping!!

Preheat oven to 150 fan 170 electric or gas 4

30 x 20cm tin (approx) greased and lined in the base with baking parchment.

350g plain flour
1 rounded teasp. bicarbonate soda
1 rounded teasp. baking powder
3 level teasp. ground ginger
150g butter
115g black treacle
115g golden syrup
230g soft brown sugar
270ml milk
1 large egg - beaten
Chopped stem ginger (optional) 3 or 4 pieces

1. Sieve together the first 4 ingredients.
2. Stir in the chopped ginger if using.
3. In a largish bowl warm together in the microwave the sugar, treacle, syrup and butter. Mix well. Allow to cool.
4. Warm the milk and add to the beaten egg.
5. Combine all the ingredients, mixing to a very soft consistency.
6. Pour into the prepared tin and cook for about 1 hour. If firm to the touch it will be ready.
7. If cooking too quickly lower the temperature slightly.
8. Leave for 5 minutes in the tin and then remove to a wire rack to cool completely.

9. Cut into squares and store in an air-tight tin to keep moist.

CHOCOLATE CHIP MUFFINS

Preheat oven 180C fan 200 electric or 6 gas

10 muffin cases in a muffin or patty tin

300g plain flour
2 rounded teasp. baking powder
100g caster sugar
250ml milk at room temperature
60g melted butter
1 large egg
1 teasp. vanilla essence
150gm white chocolate chopped into small pieces
150gm dark chocolate as above

1. Sieve the flour and baking powder into a bowl and mix in the sugar.
2. In another bowl mix together the egg, milk, essence and melted butter (melt the butter in the microwave).
3. Add the milk mixture to the flour with all of the chocolate and using a metal spoon mix well together. Don't mix more than is necessary.
4. Divide the mixture between the muffin cases and bake for about 25 minutes or until golden in colour.

BLUEBERRY MUFFINS

Preheat oven - 180C fan 200C electric or 6 gas

10 muffin cases in a muffin or patty tin.

300g plain flour
2 rounded teasp. baking powder
100g soft brown sugar

250ml milk at room temperature
1 large egg
60g melted butter
½ teaspoon vanilla essence
Small tray of blueberries (100g) - washed and drained on kitchen paper.
granulated sugar to sprinkle on top

1. Sieve together into a bowl the flour and baking powder.
2. Add to this the sugar.
3. In another bowl mix together the beaten egg, milk, essence and melted butter (as for choc. chip muffins)
4. Add the liquid to the flour and mix all together with a metal spoon - don't over mix.
5. Finally fold in the blueberries gently.
6. Divide between the muffin cases.
7. Sprinkle with granulated sugar.
8. Bake for 20 - 25 minutes till brown.

SHORTBREAD

Preheat oven 140C fan 160C electric or 3 gas

2 lightly greased baking trays

These quantities will make 2 rounds.
If you find it difficult to roll out and handle 2 rounds make individual biscuits (at stage 4) by rolling small pieces of the mix in your hands and flattening a little between the palms. Place on the baking tray and press flat with the back of a fork, obviously leaving them as thick as a biscuit should be!

300g plain flour
200g butter (at room temperature)
100g caster sugar
½ teasp. vanilla essence

1. Cream together the butter and sugar with the essence in a processor, with a mixer or by hand with a wooden spoon until light and pale.
2. Add the sieved flour and mix in till all are blended together.
3. Form into a flattened lump and wrap in cling film - place in the fridge for 20 minutes.
4. Divide the mix into 2 and on a floured surface and with a floured rolling pin, roll each half into a round. This is made easier by rolling each piece into a ball before rolling it out and also to keep the round shape keep turning the shortbread round as you roll it.
5. The circle should measure about 20cm across and be fairly thin - about ¾cm.
6. Lightly grease a flat baking tray and slide the shortbread off the work-top and onto this or gently lift with 2 slices. It doesn't matter if it breaks up a little as it can soon be joined together again with the fingers.
7. With the forefinger and thumb of your right hand go around the edge nipping it up to form a ridge. Then go around again, nipping the edge but then twisting towards the centre to create a *crimp* all the way round.
8. Prick over the centre with a fork.
9. Place in the fridge for 30 minutes to harden a little.
10. Cook for about 25 - 30 minutes till lightly golden.
11. Allow to cool for 2 minutes and then cut into pieces with a large sharp knife.
12. With a slice lift off gently to a wire rack to cool off completely.
13. Keep in an airtight container.

CHOCOLATE CARAMEL SQUARES

A great favourite with my two boys - supplied by their *Gangy* (Grandma). When cubs and camping in the New Forest at Wilverley enclosure she delivered two trays of this delectable *biscuit come cake* which were much appreciated by all their fellow campers!

Preheat the oven to 140Cfan 160C electric or 3 gas

Approx. 20cm x 30cm x 2cm(deep) greased baking tin

Biscuit base
340g plain flour
170g butter
85g caster sugar

Caramel centre
1 tin (379g) condensed milk
225g caster sugar
225g butter
2 tabsp. golden syrup

Chocolate topping
200g good plain chocolate

1. All ingredients for the base can be placed in a food processor and given short bursts until all comes together. By hand make as shortbread recipe steps 1 and 2 minus the vanilla essence.
2. Partly roll this out before lifting (roll round the rolling pin if it helps) onto the greased tray and finally pushing it to the edges by hand making sure that it is even in depth all over.
3. Bake for about 25 minutes till pale and golden and leave in the tin to cool
4. Caramel - Place all the ingredients in a saucepan and whilst stirring bring slowly to the boil. Boil gently for 7 minutes, stirring continuously on low heat. Allow to

cool.
5. When caramel is cold spread it over the biscuit base.
6. The caramel might need a short burst in the fridge to set off.
7. Break the chocolate into a bowl and melt it with short bursts in the microwave. Be careful not to heat it too much otherwise it will be ruined.
8. Spread the chocolate in a thin layer over the caramel.
9. Cut into squares before the chocolate is quite set.
10. Store in an airtight container in a cool place.

FLAPJACK - oaty and buttery!

Preheat oven 150C fan 170C electric or 4 gas

20cm x 30cm baking tray (at least 2cm deep) greased and lined with baking parchment.

230g soft brown sugar
170g butter
2 tablespoons golden syrup
340g porridge oats

1. Place the sugar, butter and syrup in a large bowl and heat in the microwave until the butter is liquid. Mix all together well.
2. Add the oats and mix in well
3. Spread evenly in the prepared tin. To help in levelling it off use the back of a wet spoon.
4. Bake for about 20 minutes and then check that it isn't browning too quickly - it may need turning if browning too much on one side.
5. It will probably take another 15 minutes to cook but if it's browning too quickly turn the heat down to 110C fan 130C electric or 2 gas. Overcooked it will be rather brittle - it is much better if a little chewy.
6. 3 minutes after removing from the oven, mark it into pieces as this will be difficult when cold.

7. Keep in an airtight container.

CHOCOLATE BROWNIES

Preheat oven 140C fan 160C electric or 3 gas

Baking tray - 20cm x 30cm - lined with non stick baking paper

350g dark chocolate (not cooking chocolate)
250g butter
3 large eggs
1 teasp. vanilla essence
250g soft brown sugar
85g plain flour
1 rounded teaspoon baking powder
100g chopped walnuts (optional)

1. Break the chocolate into pieces and place in a bowl with the butter. Melt in the microwave - checking frequently so that you catch the chocolate just as it has melted. Mix well.
2. Whisk the eggs till pale and frothy and then add the sugar and vanilla essence, whisking till thick and glossy.
3. Fold the melted chocolate and butter into the eggs and sugar.
4. Sift flour and baking powder together and with the walnuts stir into the mixture.
5. Put in prepared tin - level out.
6. Bake for 34 - 40 minutes until a knife or cocktail stick, when prodding the cake, comes out fairly clean. It is a gooey cake so a few bits are bound to stick!
7. Allow to cool in the tin on a wire rack.
8. After about one hour it should be easier to cut it into squares.
9. When storing, place a sheet of cling film between each layer to prevent sticking.

ROCK CAKES

Preheat oven to 180C fan 200C electric or 6 gas

A lightly greased baking tray

230g self raising flour
1 rounded teasp. baking powder
½ teasp. ground nutmeg (optional)
85g butter
85g demerara sugar
115g dried fruit (I prefer sultanas!)
1 large egg
A little milk (approx. 2 tablespoons)

1. Sieve flour, baking powder and ground nutmeg together.
2. Cut the butter into small pieces and rub into the flour mixture as if making scones (see next recipe)
3. Beat the egg with 1 tablespoon of milk and tip into the mix, bringing together with a fork. Add more milk if you think it is needed because it is difficult to add when the mix has fully come together! The mix needs to be quite stiff to produce the 'rocky appearance of the cakes.
4. This amount should make 12. Drop the mixture in rough dollops onto the baking tray.
5. Sprinkle with brown sugar
6. Bake for 15 - 20 minutes until nicely browned.
7. Remove to a wire rack to cool.

SCONES

Preheat the oven 200C fan 220C electric 7 gas

Baking tray lightly greased

FRUIT SCONES - add 50gm sultanas when adding the sugar.

230g self raising flour
2 rounded teasp. baking powder
55g butter
55g caster sugar
1 large egg
100ml milk (a little under)

1. Sieve together the flour and baking powder
2. Cut the butter into small pieces and then very lightly with the tips of the fingers rub into the flour.
3. Stir in the sugar
4. Whisk most of the milk together with the egg and add to the flour mix, gently bringing all together with a fork. The mixture shouldn't be too dry so add the rest of the milk if needed.
5. Gently bring altogether with the hands and turn out onto a floured surface.
6. If you have no round cutters, mould into a ball and then flatten it out on the baking tray and with a knife mark into portions as if it were a cake - not cutting right through.
7. If using cutters, roll out to about 3cm thick, cut out and place on the tray
8. Collect the pieces up and mould together. Roll out and cut out some more.
9. Brush the top with milk and bake for 15 - 20 minutes, turning heat down if browning too quickly.
10. Remove to a wire tray to cool.

CHEESE SCONES

Same oven temperatures as above.

230g self raising flour
2 rounded teasp. baking powder
1 rounded teasp. English mustard powder or ready made which can be mixed into the milk

30g butter
85g grated mature cheddar cheese
1 egg
100ml milk (a little under maybe)

1. Sieve the flour, baking powder and mustard powder altogether.
2. Proceed as for plain scones except at 3 where instead of sugar - add the grated cheese and if using ready mixed mustard mix this with the milk.
3. As well as brushing the tops with milk sprinkle over a little grated cheese which will be extra to the 85gm in the recipe.
4. Bake for 15-20 minutes. Remove to a wire tray to cool.

DROP SCONES (SCOTCH PANCAKES)

Sweet as a teatime treat or minus the sugar for savoury toppings. Delicious with just butter.

175g self raising flour
1 rounded teasp. baking powder
30g caster sugar
30g butter - melted to liquid (microwave!)
1 large egg
200ml milk + 2 tabsp.

1. Sieve the flour and baking powder together.
2. Whisk the egg and milk together and then whisk in the melted butter.
3. Place the dry ingredients in a bowl and in the centre make a largish hollow.
4. Pour some of the liquid into the centre and with a whisk gradually mix in some of the flour. Repeat this 3 or 4 times until all has been mixed together.

Hints

Use a spoon dipped in hot water to measure out

Cake testing —

Sponge or light cakes.
Lightly press the flat of your finger on top —
It is cooked if the mix springs back.
A fruit or more solid cake can be tested with a small, pointed and thin bladed knife. Pushed into the centre it should come out free of mixture.

5. Place a non-stick frying pan on the heat and when hot add a dribble of sunflower oil. With a scrunched up kitchen towel very carefully wipe the oil around the pan
6. Taking a tablespoon filled with the mix, drop gently into the hot pan - you should be able to get about 4 in.
7. At this stage you should turn the heat down a little.
8. After a couple of minutes the pancakes will bubble and be ready to turn over.
9. Cook for one minute on the other side.
10. Remove to a tea towel and keep wrapped up so that they don't dry out.
11. Oil the pan between each lot and get the pan hot to start with.

OAT SNAP BISCUITS

220g butter at room temperature
220g soft brown sugar
165g plain flour
2 rounded teasp. baking powder
220g porridge oats

Preheat oven 160C fan 180C electric or 4 gas

2 lightly greased baking trays.

1. In a bowl cream together the butter and sugar - by hand with a wooden spoon or with a mixer and beater attachment.
2. Sieve together the flour and baking powder and mix in all the remaining ingredients until they come together.
3. This should make about 24 small biscuits. Halve the mixture, halve each half and halve that again and then each remaining piece should be divided roughly into three! If this sounds like gobbledygook to you then perhaps you'll find a simpler way!
4. Roll each piece into a ball in your hands and as you place it on the baking tray press it flat with 2 fingers.
5. Bake for about 20 minutes until browned a little.

6. Remove to a wire cooling rack.
7. Store in an airtight tin.

MELTING MOMENTS (BISCUITS)

Preheat oven 160C fan 180C electric or 4 gas

340g plain flour
2 rounded teasp. baking powder
220g butter at room temperature
170g soft brown sugar

1. Repeat the method as for the oat snaps, adding the essence at the start. There aren't any oats in these biscuits but finish them off before putting them in the oven by rolling the balls in oats before flattening on the baking tray.
2. Store in an airtight tin.

RASPBERRY BUNS

Preheat oven 160C fan 180C electric or 4 gas

200g self raising flour
1 rounded teaspoon of baking powder
75g butter (at room temperature)
75g granulated sugar
1 egg
2 tablespoons of milk
½ teaspoon of vanilla essence
raspberry jam (or strawberry, blackcurrant, bramble etc)

1. Sieve the flour and baking powder together.
2. In a bowl, add the butter cut into small pieces.
3. With the tips of your fingers gently rub the fat into the flour until you have a sandy texture.
4. Add the sugar and stir in with a fork.

5. Beat the egg, milk and vanilla essence together and add to the flour mixture.
6. Mix all together with a fork till evenly mixed. Add a little more milk if very stiff.
7. Divide into about ten pieces and form into balls by rolling on the work top.
8. Place on a greased baking tray well spaced out.
9. Flatten slightly, make a hollow in the centre of each and fill with about ½ teaspoon of jam.
10. Sprinkle with granulated sugar.
11. Bake for 15 - 20 minutes and then remove to a wire cooling rack.

RECIPE INDEX

Meals for One
Meaty egg noodles	19
Tuna pasta	18

Soups and Snacks
Beefburgers	30
Carrot and orange soup	27
Cheeseburgers	30
Cheese and onion soup	24
Cheese pudding	33
Cream of mushroom soup	26
Green pea and Black Forest ham soup	25
French stick with roasted vegetables & cheese	29
Ham, mushroom & cheese omelette	31
Jacket potatoes	28
Muffin Pizzas	33

Vegetables, Potatoes, Salads & Dressings
Bakers potatoes	41
Coleslaw	50
Fry-pan baked potatoes with bacon	40
Jacket potatoes - filled	42
Mediterranean roast vegetables	38
Potato parcels	42
Potato salad	49
Rice Salad	48
Salad dressing - family friendly	44
French	45
honey and mustard	46
Spiced red cabbage with apple	36
Spicy potato wedges	39
Tomato salad	49
Winter roast vegetables	37

Pizza, Pasta, Rice, Savoury Pancakes & Tarts
Caribang (cabbage, rice and bangers!)	58
Gruyere cheese tart	62
Macaroni cheese with ham	54

Pancake parcels with ham and cheese	60
Pizza	52
Rice - plain and pilaff	85
Roast vegetable and sausage pasta	56
Sausage, bacon and cheddar risotto	59
Savoury tart with mozzarella (and filling of choice)	63
Smoked fish, mushroom and pasta bake	55
Spaghetti with egg and bacon sauce	64

Main Meals
FISH

Fish parcels	71
Fish pie	69
Kedgeree	66
Oven baked (one dish) fish	72
Salmon fish cakes	68

MEAT

Cassoulet	91
Chicken curry	94
Chilli con carne	85
Corned beef hash with fried eggs	97
Cottage pie	81
Crispy chicken with tomato dip	102
Beef casserole	93
Lamb hot pot	96
Lasagne	79
Meat balls in tomato sauce	87
Meat loaf	90
Moussaka	83
Multi-purpose savoury mince (bulk recipe)	74
Multi-purpose savoury mince (single recipe)	78
Pork and barley bake	92
Pork casserole	93
Rice - plain and pilaff	85
Roast chicken, gravy and roast potatoes	103
Sausage and onion batter (toad in the hole)	95
Savoury pancakes with cheese sauce	84
Spaghetti bolognaise	80
Spring rolls with dipping sauce	100

Stuffed peppers	82
Sweet and sour pork	98
Toad in the hole	95

Food for Friends
Beef stroganoff	107
Breaded pork escalopes with ham and cheese	110
Braised lamb shanks in red wine	115
Chicken saltimbocca	114
Salmon en croute	111
Spare-rib pork chops in cider and cream sauce	112

Sweets, puddings etc.
Apple batter	127
Apple pie	133
Baked cheesecake	129
Bakewell tart	130
Banoffi pie	118
Bread and butter pudding	128
Caramelised upside down fruit tart (tart tatin)	125
Caramel sauce for icecream	121
Chocolate sauce for icecream	121
Chocolate mousse	123
Fresh fruit ripple	122
Fruit sponge	134
Lemon delight	126
Orange cheesecake	119
Sauces for icecream - caramel and chocolate	121
Sherry trifle	124
Shortbread fruit tart	119
Syrup sponge pudding	135
Vanilla icecream	120

Pastry, Cakes and Biscuits
Blueberry muffins	144
Butter cream	138
Carrot cake	142
Chocolate brownies	149
Chocolate chip muffins	144
Chocolate fridge cake	140

Cup cakes	139
Drop scones (Scotch pancakes)	152
Fairy cakes	139
Flapjack	148
Ginger cake 1	143
Melting moments (biscuits)	155
Oat snap biscuits	154
Pastry - puff, filo, short, flan and sweet	136/137
Raspberry buns	155
Rock cakes	150
Scones - plain, sultana and cheese	150/151
Shortbread	145
Sponge cake	138